INVITATION TO THE REVOLUTION OF A SOUL

ATHENS 2016

For those who measure time in smiles, not minutes

*For those who let art blaze new trails in their soul
so they can reach those parts of hers
they don't own yet*

INVITATION TO THE REVOLUTION OF A SOUL

Copyright © 2015 by Angelos Michalopoulos
All rights reserved

Translation: Angelos Michalopoulos,
              Andreas Machairas
Paintings: Angelos Michalopoulos,
Photography: George Sideris,
              Vangelis Pelekanakis,
              Zoe Michalopoulou

© Angelos Michalopoulos, 2015.
This publication (work, material, book) may not be reproduced, transmitted or copied in part or in whole, by any means and in any form, nor may it be translated, adapted, adjusted, converted, or otherwise circulated or communicated to the public in any way or by any means, in accordance with the provisions of L. 2121/1993 and the Berne Convention for the Protection of Literary and Artistic Works, without the prior written approval of the author.
The reproduction of the typesetting and layout, the cover and the overall aesthetic appearance of this book by photocopying, electronic or any other methods for purposes of exploitation is strictly prohibited according to article 51 of L. 2121/1993.

(The publication, reproduction, transmission or exploitation of this book in part or in whole without the written permission of the copyright holder is strictly prohibited)

www.angelosm.com
email: onelilo@angelosm.com

Printed by Nota All About Print, www.notadd.gr

ISBN: 978-618-82378-5-8

I learned though, before they began talking to me,
how to hear what they didn't want to tell me
(Turn over your silence to find out what you really want to say)..18

2. How much I like the stories you tell my fairytales!
(The part of my character that was always able to fit
in that interval between midnight and the first doubt of the day) 20

3. Drinking two gulps of your truth
I discovered that I will never be able to taste the flavor of your conscience
(Your thoughts forgot again today to take their contraceptive)..22

4. Come on, wear the love you are feeling!
(How many times today did you let your life kiss you on the mouth?)...23

5. The day I persuaded my mind to try to convince me
that I am better than my reality
(My mistakes are ready to start altering right away my incoming victory).......................................24

6. I am afraid that pretty soon I will no longer entirely fit
in the accidental miracle I've become
(Living a life that never wanted to know its true dimensions)..26

7. The older I get, the more I become the illegitimate
child of the risks I take in order to be happy
(Where did I learn to be the favorite child
of the one decision in my life I cannot make?)...28

8. Can I tell you how I became the bill
I will soon have to present to my happiness?
(What I feel looking at the bad check
my character flaws just wrote to my future)..29

9. I stand in between my heart and my logic
to prevent her light my happiness from dirtying the former
(I became the person who no longer fits in what he wants to say) 30

10. When a person lets his smartest ambiguity define him
(Walking towards the spot of your brain
where tomorrow has already begun to fall in love with my character flaws)..................................33

11. Those advantages of mine I found
when I managed to cut one of my mistakes in two
(What I learned interrupting my silence while she was talking)...34

12. Silences know how to ask the best questions
(Every important painting knows how to hide within it
the many smudges that gave birth to it)..

so we can see from which part of our vanities we've made you
(The spot in a marriage where smiles don't dare to go anymore)..38

15. The time has come for me to no longer fear those emotional paths
that will never let me return to where I started
(Enthusiasm is what remains in a man
when his inner beauty suddenly decides to kiss him on the mouth)..40

16. I wish I could remember in which pocket of my soul
I hid last summer's most beautiful day
(Why do I insist all these years on living a soul away
from my favorite embrace?)..42

17. My self-confidence just decided to buy me from my own mistakes
(From all the possible endings of my sorrow
I picked the one I understood the least) 44

18. How beautiful the day is during which
my joy kisses me at least once on the mouth!
(Why should I be condemned to live constantly
a shortcoming away from my best self?) 45

19. So happy you can sing with your mouth closed
(What I feel every time I plant a beautiful thought
in the middle of my ugliest word)...47

20. The part of myself I did not insert
in the farewell letter I wrote to my innocence
(What liberates me from the person I can't afford to become?) 50

21. Why did all that I've failed to achieve in my life
never stop writing bad checks
to everything I've already achieved?
(I never dared ask my victories the reason they respect me less than my defeats) 52

22. I would be really unhappy
if I ever lost my ability to shudder
(A heart becomes more beautiful
when she decides on her own to open the door to the unknown
without ever having knocked on it) 54

23. In the disappointment for my defeat
I began to curse at the dice that live permanently in my mind,
the ones I use every time to make the decisions
I cannot make using only my own capabilities
(When will I stop injecting myself
with vaccines against my happiness?)..55

26. I was always partial to that part of your character
    that wanted to live crammed between my heart and your sorrow
    (I built a trust from a caress that wants to lie only to its owner
    and from two thoughts of mine that for some time now
    refuse to answer my honesty's questions
    I began to build a compassion) 59

27. The day I became the superfluous enemy of my own memory
    (The world would be a more beautiful place
    if we could all trust the shyest dream we hide inside us)..

28. Kissing on the mouth every character flaw of mine
    that has not insisted on introducing itself to me yet
    (Is there a right dosage of conscience?)..63

29. This must be the point in one's life
    when the various full stops he occasionally placed in his happiness
    decide to charge him and start rebuilding him from scratch
    (If your mistakes come to love you it's forever)..64

30. Why should the redemption of an ugliness be the apology of beauty?
    (Could this be the way a self-confidence hides its biggest fears
    in the cowardice of its owner?) 65

31. It's time to stop stopping
    (Am I worthy to add to my life
    what I don't know how to remove from it?)..66

32. How I reached the edge of my last ego
    without knowing if there's a next one further on
    (I can no longer stand living inside those truths
    that insist I must suffer to learn how to reach their end) ....

33. In love with those sins of my life that wish to remain invisible
    (When was the last time you spoke with a dream of yours
    that does not want to wake up next to you?)...70

34. Touching the end of my most incomplete truth
    I started remaking my soul out of the thousands of emotions
    I never found the courage to feel
    (If you want to figure out how your happiness works
    try to find out who your meanness wants you to be)..

35. What makes you think that my tears can explain to you
    the reason why I'm miserable?
    (Watching my originality self-congratulating herself
    for the fire she just started inside my brain) 73

(How I wish while I'm arguing with the person I love
I were able to understand which part of my character I am trying to defeat) 78

38. Letting my next words rip out my compassion from inside me
to deliver it to the doorstep of your truth
(Maybe this is the way a fog reveals any darkness
it can no longer stand hiding inside it)..80

39. How "almost" ended up being the second most expensive word in the world
(Do you have the impression that "if" will ever want
to relinquish its primacy?) 82

40. Is this the crossroads in my life
where my logic and my soul decide to follow different directions?
(The day lies stopped admiring the dark side of their owners)..84

41. I step into the ring to fight my vanity
knowing that if I ever manage to win
I will become more radiant than I can bear
(How will I manage, out of all these mistakes I see in front of me,
to make the one that is the least expensive?)...86

42. Wearing that ego of mine which every time I lose
pretends it doesn't know me
(What I felt listening to the night read my life's story
as loudly as it could in front of my fears)..87

43. A revolution begins the moment man decides
to break free of his shackles and go where his soul already is
(The strongest prison bars in the world are made of these thoughts
that will never become deeds) 90

44. How did I end up being a hostage of the smartest question I can ask my own life?
(Perhaps because I will never get away
from the dumbest answer I give to the one question
my ego doesn't stop asking me)..92

45. A teardrop is just another promise man makes to his truth
knowing that he will never honor it
(Why do I call dream the part of my soul I will never be able to touch?)...........................94

46. When you feel that your happiness has detached herself from your soul
and has begun to walk away from you to try to seek the protection of your ambiguity
(I will never stop defending my future
from the attacks of that sorrow of mine that insists on living only in my past)..................96

| | learned how to grab me from my vanity
and throw me on that shortcoming of mine
that wants to humiliate me in front of everything I don't know) .... 100 |
| --- | --- |
| 49. | Listening to the velvet sound of a silence
that pleads with me to let it try to conquer on
its own the soul of the person I love
(The decadence of a man lives forever
among those brilliant words of his he left unsaid) .... 102 |
| 50. | The scarecrow I installed in the middle of my truth
to scare away bigger truths just submitted its resignation
(Since we broke up only in total darkness can I stand any longer
to touch my character flaws) .... 104 |
| 51. | I am not stupid enough to be obsessed with how smart I am
(I might not be unhappy enough to be constantly concerned with my happiness) .... 105 |
| 52. | Pessimism of mine, will you please stop selling me to my next sorrow?
(The long lost pieces of my character
that I found while smashing the glass display window of my logic) .... 107 |
| 53. | My defeats know me better than I know myself
(What I learned by forgetting how to listen to the echo of my victories) .... 109 |
| 54. | The ambitious fog anxiously tries to find in which part of my insecurities
it could live so that it could offer me more of its services
(Don't worry, in my life I was always careful
not to be happier than my happiness) .... 112 |
| 55. | Doing the best I can not to locate
the shortest century of sorrow that lives inside me
(Is there a full stop that does not want to be perfect anymore?) .... 116 |
| 56. | This is how a soul that just managed to lose the last emotion
she had in her feels
(How many fewer things would you have liked to know about yourself?) .... 118 |
| 57. | The day I let myself be defined by the success of my own failures
(This is how I became the ungrateful smile of an optimism
that openly hates my born-again cowardice) .... 120 |
| 58. | I live in a reality that always has a sweet flavor to spare
(Let me share with you what I learned repairing my backup self-confidence) .... 122 |
| 59. | I tossed a paradise in the deepest garbage can
that was washed up in front of my feet
by a sea wave that wanted to be something less than blue
(Could this be another one of my failed efforts to sell you pieces of myself
I can't deny are mine anymore?) .... 123 |

62. Why do I continue after all those years every morning
    to fall in love again with the part of my happiness
    I never understood?
    (Why should I start fixing my age when it hasn't broken down yet?)...130

63. The last step of every voyage I made
    was the first step of a journey into my own soul
    (Tell my why does a loneliness always want to end with a kiss
    that does not know why it exists?)..131

64. Why does my happiness have to be the favorite shooting range
    where my lies practice their aim?
    (What I learned trying to free myself
    from my honesty's opinion of me)...134

65. Can you please show me what you fought tooth and nail
    not to reveal to your mirror a few minutes ago?
    (Trying to detach myself from the thousands of promises
    I've made from time to time to my own body) 135

66. So, are these the favors my shadow asks of you
    to leave you alone?
    (What you just saw are the emotions,
    or rather the explosives my childhood hid
    in my soul's main square)..

67. In every step I take I carry on my back
    the part of God I never believed in
    (All that the pockets that were born full and over time emptied
    have to confess to their owner) 139

68. Looking into your eyes
    I realized what I'm asking the back side of my smile to deliver to you
    (When I decided to hide in the questions of a winter
    which searches through the happiness of the most miserable person living in it
    to find the spot in spring where it will place its last day)..

69. The day when for the first time I reached the brink of darkness
    and decided not to stop but keep on walking
    (Will I ever learn, I wonder, what "minimum courage" means?)..144

70. I cheat on my truth with the best friend of the flipside of my life
    (The part of my dignity that my ego considers superfluous) 146

71. Why does every new kind of truth you discover
    contain two kinds of delusion so you can pick the one you despise the least?
    (Watching the abyss that permanently lives in my heart
    leak drop by drop all the black its brightest side does not need)..147

74. What you owe to those smiles of yours
    that are born from golden dead ends
    (Let me give you the part of my victory
    I had to share with my defeatism)..153

75. Taking aimless strolls in the parts of my mind
    I never learned how to dominate
    (The most beautiful flowers often grow in soil
    people spat at every time they went by)...155

76. The man who cultivates pains in those fields inside his brain
    that always belonged to his richest fogs
    (No matter what season it is
    I am trying to always keep at least one day of spring inside me) 156

77. Trying to determine how capable
    an ambassador of my soul I've become
    (This is how I learned to defeat my identity)..158

78. Did you notice that our truth for the first time ever
    refused to be with us in the picture we just took?
    (Is it time, I wonder, to invite my luck to dinner?) 161

79. At the limits of where my soul can reach to paint
    every time she stretches her imagination so far that she surpasses reality
    lives the tyranny of not knowing which part of my normality
    I should blow up to search in its ruins
    for that flame my passion will use to remake me from scratch
    (If my life knew how not to fear white
    she wouldn't wear black)..164

80. In few things is man better
    than in making invisible cages for himself
    which he will rush to enter as soon as the back side
    of his self-confidence unlocks the door for him
    (What is the address of your favorite insecurity?) 166

81. When I stopped stealing questions
    from the pocket of tomorrow's happiness
    (I don't ask my malfunctions to explain what every new defeat means to me anymore) 168

82. The part of my life I cannot see
    each time I stand at the very end of my self-confidence
    watching my mistakes trying to find a way to spawn new mistakes
    (Trying to find out how a sorrow
    that never asked me to tell it why it started ends) ....

(What I learned while trying to convince myself
that the defeats of my brain are not also my defeats)..172

85. Those nights that, to be able to go to sleep,
a few minutes before every midnight
I end up giving my self-confidence a new name
(In love with any emotions of mine
that right at that minute I couldn't afford to feel) 174

86. The part of my happiness that I can't understand
why it wants to make me happy
(Wrapped around those phrases of yours
which for some time now I can't understand what they are trying to hide from me) 175

87. My sorrow is the astray I've been using for years to extinguish my sunshines in
(I'll agree with what you say,
if you are able to convince me that you are smarter than your fears)...177

88. I kept on throwing my sorrow's trash
in front of the last emergency exit my happiness had
until I managed to block it completely
(It was a time when my life didn't feature upcoming battles,
only future successes that didn't know how to be happy)..1

89. Do you know what it is like to live imprisoned in absolute freedom?
(Please come and embrace me with those emotions of yours
that you don't know yet how to feel) 181

90. To avoid becoming my next sorrow
I became the last version of my happiness
(Could this be a point in my life when I can measure everything
except my own dimensions?)...183

91. Did the sky ever realize how many sunshines went through it today?
(Did I ever realize how many happy moments went through me today?) 185

92. Embracing the fog that comes out of your self-discipline
I fell in love with the front side of my own cowardice
(If you were to bump into the first minute of your previous sorrow
what you would you say to it?)...188

93. Death is man's liberation from his own freedom
(The day we began to make a joy out of all the blue
the sky didn't need at the time to convince itself that it had no clouds in it)...............190

96. Picking up from the floor of our stupidity
    any of our defeats that didn't manage to become guilt
    (Is this the person I was before I met my ego?) 196

97. Unfortunately I just discovered
    that my ambiguity is pregnant with my smile
    (I wish I knew what my laughter believes about me) ....

98. The time has come for me to feel what I already believe in
    (I'm really afraid that my truth will soon start lying to me) ....

99. I turned my mind over to see who its manufacturer is
    (I hope that my sorrow will be the last emotion in my life
    to learn how to be happy) 200

100. Watching my self-criticism frantically search in my past
     to find proof of who I'll become
     (Trapped in what's left of my freedom
     if I take away its right to judge me) 202

101. Counting the currency his sorrow
     will use to buy him from the next hour of his life
     (The moment he realized that he had mistakenly
     entered somebody else's shadow) 204

102. My remorse just warned me that from now on
     it will spawn inside me its own defeats whenever it wants to
     (I began to pick up from the floor what was left of those looks
     which my image has been giving me for some time now) 206

103. I caught my silences selling my secrets one by one
     to your biggest character flaws
     (I just gave permission to my cowardice to sink right outside your passion) 208

104. Playing on a throw of the dice
     the apology I owe to my future
     (Each mistake likes to create a minimal conscience
     which it will donate to its owner during the first minute of the next lost battle) 210

105. Don't ever try to find out which parts of your kindness
     your malice uses to make herself more attractive than your verbal punches
     (Beds are not made by people, they are made by their consciences) 211

106. Man can go mad when he realizes
     that from now on he must live in the same mind
     with those thoughts of his he can no longer think
     (When did I start transforming every dream of mine
     into the safe haven where I can hide from my own self?) ....

   for a way to become more black)..216

109. I no longer know whether I am the customer or the product
   (Once in a while the sun rises from inside a smile
   that had been always told by everyone that it was born expired) 217

110. Now that I reached the end of my happiness,
   the time has come for me to start seducing one by one my own beliefs
   (The odyssey of a self-confidence
   that never believed in the stupidity of its owner) 218

111. The dimensions of a smile that doesn't feel the need to end
   (Beauty has the courage of ten uglinesses) 220

112. When my truth discovered the comfort
   my lies are supplying my life with
   (How few things about you does the paradise
   you built in the center of your brain actually know!)... 222

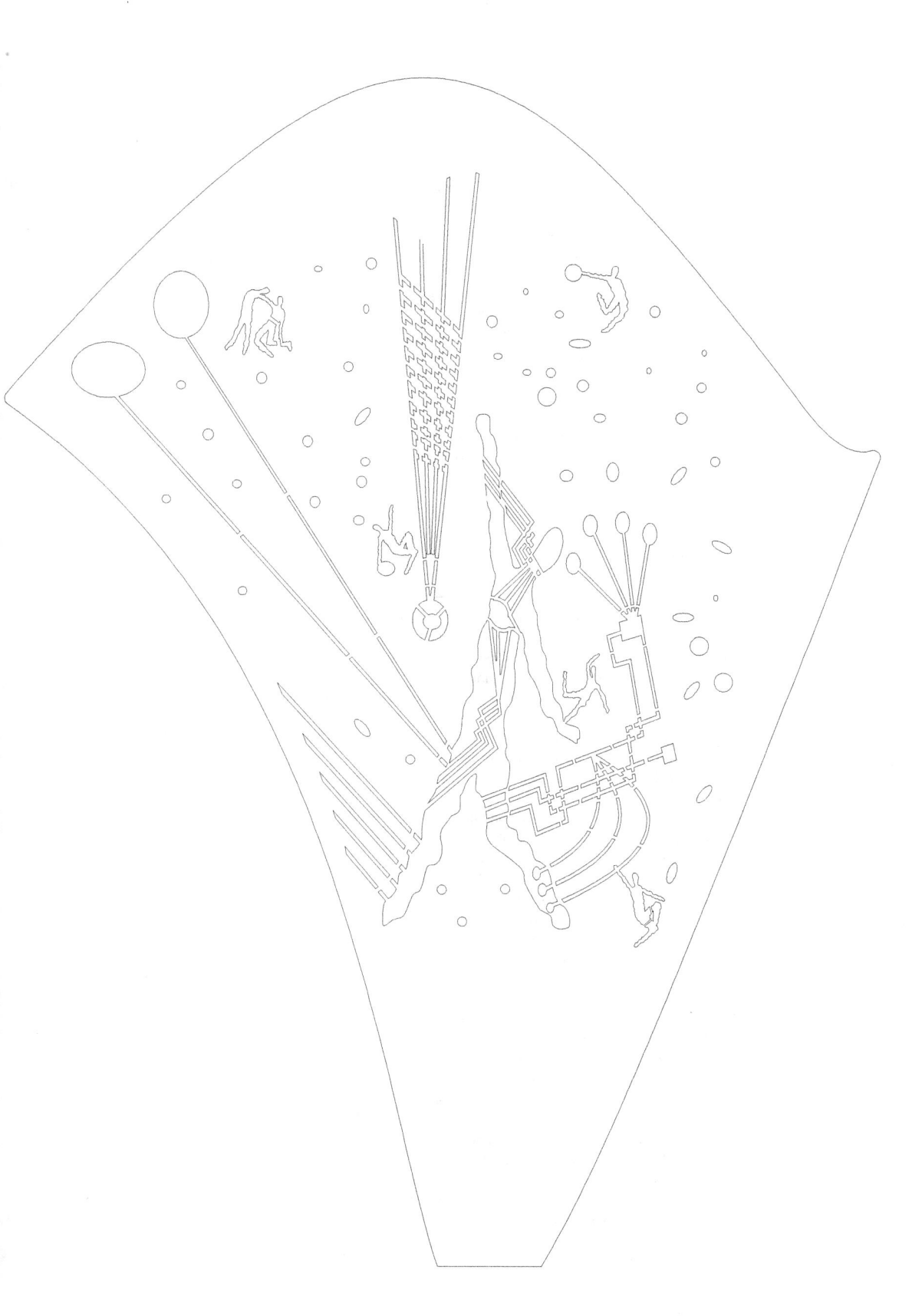

I beg you, don't try anymore
to make me embrace my authenticity today.
The poor thing, since it still doesn't feel comfortable when we are all alone,
has left my side for a while so it won't breathe,
won't feel the flavor of my words
as they rush out of my mouth to meet their destiny.

I always believed that man can look at his past
for the first time without being embarrassed
when he admits that his fist and his stupidity
are the strengths that got him to where he is today.
Well, as if they knew it,
for the past few minutes they both have me standing three feet away from them
and are ready to prove to me how weak I become
each time I feel stronger than I actually am.

An old tear of mine had once told me
before it dried out on the surface of the reality I forced it to experience:
"Let your biggest shortcoming show you
how clever your stupidity will allow you to become".
Do you think I've reached that point in time again
when the ugliness of my life must realize what it owes my delusions?
I don't have the slightest idea.
Do you think that's why a tear is the tax
my stupidity must pay reality from time to time
so it will allow me to advance to the next minute of my life safe and sound?

Trying to find my sorrow a second job
for when I don't force her to take care of me,
I became the beggar of my favorite mediocrity.
My hope, trying to find out where they sell sunbeams,
new, used -it doesn't make a difference-
because the ones she had ran out,
exhausted starts sinking after a while
in the stunningly beautiful disappointment I gave her long ago as a gift.
It's this disappointment I made out of thousands of dreams
that never managed to find the different kinds of truth
I had installed in them so they can become reality.
It's this prefabricated reality
that urges me to become the last available deserter of my courage
who thinks he is hounded by any emotion of his
that still hasn't learned how to be disappointed.

What have I to offer to all that's happening to me
which I can no longer understand?
What have I to offer now to the relationship
my image has developed for the past several sorrows
with my most inexplicable darkness?

it began to ritually unfold leaving it before my feet
urging the cynical beauty of black
to swallow all the questions the soil of the earth around me wanted to ask me.

How much honesty does a darkness contain
that wants to honor the reason it exists,
and perhaps also the very past it was born in!
Instantly my life got flooded with a different kind of past than mine,
a past which commanded me to immediately start trying to unfasten my fears
one by one from their place of birth.
It wanted me to let them climb up to my throat
so they can evaporate along with my next breath, my next sigh, my next word,
in the breeze which this afternoon is especially eager to take them far away
so I won't see them again before me for years, maybe never.

In the almost toxic but inexplicably beautiful fumes of this darkness
I was able for the first time in my life
to see clearly what my soul's signature looks like
and thus ensure that she is the one who actually signs every time my logic looks away
on the lower right corner of every blank page my life brings before her.
Will I be able today to figure out the difference
between the actual dimensions of my soul
and those my self-preservation assured me for years
that it would be best if it looked at them first on my behalf before I did?
Who do I think I am anyway, daring to approach my thoughts from their back side?

Ah, how I wish I could have realized when I was young
that the cowardice of meanness
always has more weapons at its disposal than its courage!
Had I managed to do that I could have placed my rage
between what my mediocrity is afraid of
and all that my perfectionism demands of me
and, grabbing the most heavily-built limitations
I have personally imposed on my life,
I could have smashed it into a thousand pieces
to finally see what it's made of.

Perhaps this way I could figure out
where it derives this fascinating power it has
to grab from my hands my life's steering wheel whenever it feels like it
and drive my day wherever it wants.
Thus I lived for years as the most successful slave my freedom ever had,
a miserable wretch who needed every last muscle of his unhappiness
to help him hold up every minute of his life
against his truth so he can clearly see what it was made of.

Come my generous winter, stop giving me that look,
come and lean over me
and with your huge frozen ax start digging inside me to find

I offer my day every morning for what I intend to do to it
and the medals that tomorrow has already started pinning on my lapel
for all those trophies of darkness
which shortly after midnight my greed will grab me by the throat
demanding that I deliver them to it by noon.

Still not knowing who the referee is
in the fight my fears are about to start among themselves,
I begin each day constructing from scratch the key to my own failure,
the one that never wanted to learn how to fit
in the keyhole of my personal unhappiness.

Yet another day in which I won't be able to figure out
how I will be able to cope with the brilliant defeat,
which, from the time I woke up,
has been standing half a pessimism away from me
and refuses to take even one step back.

Meanwhile, the fairytales I will have to concoct during the day
to ensure that I will I reach its end as a winner
sit at the corner of the huge iron table
staring at me as if they are not afraid at all to show me
how much they detest me.
I end up, by continuing to drink the rewards that my self-defeatism
has been offering my next triumph for some time now,
letting my fingers fall in love with the texture of the night
which represents in every dawn of my life
the section of my mind that never believed in my own freedom.

I can no longer watch my soul
fall in love every morning at the breakfast table
with all the injuries I kept on donating to myself
during the course of another long night
and, as soon as it darkens, I can no longer watch the mistakes I just made
run to ask each other at which point of my enthusiasm
I abandoned the least courageous questions
I have to ask the day that is coming.

Somewhere close to midnight,
in those hours when life's indecent imperfections
really like to paint its decadence
on the insecurities of the people they dominate,
I feel as if, trying hard to impersonate an authenticity
that has the courage to be less real that its greatest lie,
I have, without realizing, climbed up onto an imposing marble pedestal.
There I stand for hours completely silent,
surrounded by the thousands of questions
which, for some reason I haven't figured out yet,
the most cowardly darkness that the night has in it
hesitates to ask me.

Trying to correct me, their gaze sets me free.
Only now am I finally able to understand
how much those moments helped me discover
all that I have to learn how to feel
to be able to stand living with myself for yet another day.

before I managed to trust it myself.
Using the light of the sunrise in your soul
I began to measure what quantity of black I can stand staring at
until I start seeing everything around me turn white.

I felt the distance separating me
from all those things in my life
my logic would never want me to realize
growing, until it became so small
that I could no longer explain it to myself,
I could only feel it.

A bit later the shyest darkness the night had in her
came dressed as a very genteel boatman
to take me to the shore on the other side,
the place where I should go so I can try to better hide
what I must eventually start looking for.
Life around me started laughing using all those fake smiles
that were left over from that night in my teens
when I learned for the first time that sometimes when you become phony
you often end up looking more like the person you always wanted to be.

I still get impressed by how different from mine
the life of some of my emotions is.
They behave as if they are seasonal tourists
who enter and leave my life depending on how good a time they are having.
They are the casual waiters who are only able to serve me my own chaos,
the ones who dare question my truth
only in the moments when she is fighting for her survival
from the attacks of the part of myself that is in love with my lies.

My emotions often have a way of making me believe
that I work exclusively for the kind of chaos I no longer represent,
this anarchy that becomes visible only in those moments of my life
during which I just fail to comprehend that I can't carry anything more on my back
beyond the weight of my self-confidence.

I never learned how to forgive
those emotions of mine I can't feel anymore
before I throw them to the part of the sky
which it has ceded to me exclusively itself so I can store there
whatever is useful only to my melancholy, not to me.

All I can do now is try to ignore everything
that is able to figure out faster than me
what that shredded into a thousand darknesses twilight is trying to tell them,
the one I personally produce daily
from the purest materials I find looking though
the unspoken words my conscience leaves behind her
every time she says "thank you" to me.

you realize that all these years
your own life never once asked to kiss you on the mouth.
You have become as weak as your smallest joy.
You have become so weak, that you have become your greatest fear.

The enormous factories of meanness located at the far back of your head
turn off their machines one by one
and you are left all alone, emotionally unarmed
at the end of an otherworldly emotional void,
surrounded by the sweet solitude of being the only person in the world
who can determine the level of ambiguity his next heartbeat will contain.
It's the hour you are no longer the small-time merchant of the essence of your life,
you don't need to buy or sell some part of yourself
to convince your self-esteem that you too are worth something.

Emboldened, you start talking to you tears about everything that scares you,
everything that cannot fit in that black second
which for days now you've been feeling wringing your neck,
just to keep on proving to you
how much more insignificant than your time you really are.
It's those moments of your life that have been following you wherever you go
constantly staying a semi-transparent guilt away
without you being able to see them.
You became the music you could never listen to,
the beauty you could never convince to slip inside you
and try to transform all the rejected, forgotten colors
that live in some dusty corner of your soul into a stunning sunset.

You immediately tried to fit who you are into the single question
that for years you've been trying to ask the part of your life
which, each day that goes by, since you don't know what else to call it,
you have been calling "my future with me".
You sat along with the late afternoon
that wanted to be more lazy than intelligent,
more rusty than glittering,
to select from the sunbeams that fall like mad rain at your feet
the ones that better match those bright yellow questions
which, to avoid killing them,
your quest for perfection ended up learning how to love.

On the way to receiving the first prize from your sorrow,
while carrying a huge pink "thank you",
you begin to slap in the face one by one your old smiles
that are standing proudly upright on your left and right to honor you.
The emotional blood that has been pointlessly circulating for hours
inside the body of your day
suddenly gave birth to the most cheerful but vulnerable scarlet answer
you ever expected to hear.

in those corners of my mind I intentionally leave poorly lit
so I can still convince myself that they are smarter than they actually are.

Thrilled with the strength of my mental arms
I began to deny myself the right to feel the tears of the full moon
which for years has been living inside me.
It's the moon that remembers how to rise
even on those nights when the sky,
suffering a sorrow even greater than mine,
removes all colors from itself except one and instantly becomes,
with the last push of the smallest insecurity I feel right then,
sadder than black.
Seeing the section of the sky which is right above me suffering,
I realize that, until I find out where the journey to my sorrow's birthplace ends
I will constantly keep on stumbling
upon the first pages of my autobiography.

My mind erases and overwrites my previous thought
until its own surface starts to tear apart,
not because of the effort, but because of the frustration.
I want to grab half the decision I am about to make from inside my cowardice
and throw it at the sunshine that still glows over the other half.
The various "don'ts" that live in a decision
that does not fear the cowardice of its owner
more than his actual strength
always try to find ways to soothe the anger it feels itself
before it rises to the edge of his lips and becomes a final act.
I am left struggling to repair, as fast as I can, the currency my logic uses
to buy off my body the qualms she has hidden inside it.

Hearing my fears whisper among themselves
right behind some lanky minced words on the tip of my lips,
I feel that the sea has started making her own nets
to catch the fish that have been forever living in her.
Is my mind perhaps trying to do the same?
My courage refuses today to obey the orders my mind gives it
and begins to break, one by one, all the promises it made yesterday,
not only to me, but also to my enthusiasm.

In the celestial storm which I personally gave birth to
using the least counterfeit spare parts of my anger
I become the favorite conversational partner
of all the choices my guilt has to annihilate me.
I am finally ready to sell the benefit of a right decision
to what the future of a wrong one thinks of me today.

The remorse of a lifetime that never understood why it suffered
rushed to enter my mouth all at once,
hoping to manage to wrap the words
I was planning to utter for some time now
around the footprints of an aged honesty
that struggles to learn new ways
to convince me that there is still space for her inside me.
I am no longer my favorite prison warden.
I am not even my favorite prisoner.

The unsuitable to my ego surprise
never stops admiring the shiny accident it knows it hides inside it.

Trying to hide from the next cry which the part of my time
that is demanding I re-live a few of its minutes for a second time wants me to utter,
I entered from the back side the shadow my courage gave me as a gift
the first moment it stopped gazing at my mediocrity
while it was looking at itself in the mirror.

My fears began again to fear me.
My next day has already learned how to detest
the transparent shape of the lie I am trying to sell it.
It's no wonder that my life's green traffic lights have already begun to question,
not only where my cowardice finds the strength to refuse to celebrate her victories,
but also where my fist finds the strength
to insist on disguising my courage as something that is less terrifying to me.

There are times when, hearing my beliefs talking in whispers among themselves
without me being able to intervene,
I begin to suspect that I am much shorter than my actual height.
Hold on, my soul!
Hold fast against what only your uncompromising, blackened fingers,
the ones I forced you for ten whole days
to keep immersed in my most ambitious darknesses,
can touch anymore.

I turned the light off as fast as I could to give myself a chance,
among the hundreds of darknesses that were in the room at the time,
to find the one that could become a good friend.
In the tremendously powerful absence of soul I felt right then
I realized that I lived in an odd kind of time interval
which, not knowing itself whether to believe in me or in my absence,
started believing in itself.

Meanwhile, the inadequacy I had been feeling for some time now
came and stood just outside the main gate of my nakedness
and looked at me heavy-eyed,
urging me to search for the one darkness around me
that during those moments wouldn't speak to anyone,
find a way to sit by its side and open up my heart to it.
Shortly after came the most carnivorous questions I have
disguised as remarkable bits of knowledge.
The scrawny "maybes" also came
masquerading as full-bodied "certainties".

As time went by, I felt the darkness that I loved the most
drying on the body of that nakedness of mine that feared me most,
I felt on my face an ever stronger draft of air
caused by the dreams that brushed by my life at breakneck speed.

I am not afraid.
I am not afraid.
In my life I've lived through midnights that lasted for months
and daybreaks that lasted for seconds.
It's those daybreaks that never wanted
to get through adolescence and become days
because they didn't believe even for a moment
all those things I promised them.
Darkness soon gave me as a gift the parts of its fist it did not need any more,
hoping I will finally find the courage to hit in the face
the tremendous personal storm which hasn't forgotten the pledge it gave me
that at some point, probably soon, it will have to come and crush me.

Tonight I'm treating all my misgivings to whatever they want to drink.
The start of my soul will accept today the marriage proposal
her own end made her years ago.
The noose will no longer seek to clutch in its hands
the least protected fringes of my dream.
Dusk tonight will not ascend to the earth
as always by way of the unbearably long downhill,
but will emerge from that spot inside me
I am no longer certain still belongs to me.

The body of the fog that forms every time a person's despairs
break into uncontrollable laughter right in front of him
suddenly decided to become totally transparent.
The feelings of guilt tonight will not only spawn midnight,
they will spawn opportunities too.
The shadows today will not only give birth to hideaways,
they will also give birth to real embraces camouflaged as mythical gates.

These are the moments in one's life that those words
that live inside the heretical nudities of a soul
which are still interested in what kind of image she will wear,
having no one else to tell,
start confiding to the nudities of a body
everything they fear themselves.
What does one have to do to learn how to forget
without feeling that each time he tries to forget something
he ends up remembering something much more important?

While I was talking to her, my nakedness suddenly lowered her zipper
and grabbed a truth that was casually passing between our bodies
certain that neither of us would pay it any notice,
as was the case for so long now.
She immediately placed it inside her, not to avoid losing it,
but so that you won't be able to discover it later on.
I wore backwards the wounds inflicted on me by the absurdity
the most carefree side of my courage has suddenly acquired
and lay down on the most unsatisfied bed
I had seen in my life.

My shortcomings had lain on it before me
hoping to convince me to become one
with what my nakedness fears most of all, my cowardice.
Maybe that's why only those damn solitudes
know how to make beds that will never feel satisfied.
Why can't I ever find the courage to defend my nakedness?
Why do I always leave it alone
to face my self-criticism's most duplicitous questions?
How much of my own cowardice
can my poor nakedness stand to always carry with it?
No more than what would make my courage feel afraid.

When I finished washing off my sorrow
all that was inflicted on her for so long
by the inappropriateness I feel each time I attack my happiness
without having all my shortcomings with me,
I started putting on my self-confidence backwards as quickly as I could
and within a minute learned many things about myself
which only my worst enemy could know.

Walking for some time between the intelligence of the gray
invented by the part of my life in which I no longer know what I must do to survive,
and the emotional essence of a day
that refuses to translate itself
into anything more than a skinny, frightened zero,
I found a spot that looked to me
emotionally more comfortable than any other.
There I sat down right away cross-legged
amid all my thoughts I couldn't produce at the time,
and after vainly dropping to my knees
and begging my laughter for hours to come again to the edge of my mouth,
I began to weep.
Happiness of mine, why do you no longer trust what my laughter confides to you?

From my misery I'm separated by two smiles and a whisper.
I can no longer afford to be the only person in the world
who continues to be wanted by the wreckage
my perpetually incomplete quest for perfection left inside me
on its way to cash in the value I always thought I had
at the pawnshop to which I went to buy back
what my self-criticism had just sold
to the counterfeit uniqueness of the story of my life.

I threw my ears at the face of the strong wind coming straight at me
so I no longer have to hear the ever unsatisfied cries of my rage
recalling me to order so they can continue teaching me
how to properly destroy my every day
before I give it a chance to ask me
the one question it has for me.

Not knowing how else to entertain my awkwardness,
I started decorating the tears I shed all these years
with the stunningly beautiful emotional naiveté
I always used to express what I was saying
except for what I really wanted to say.

From now on the colors of my life
will only use as currency my very own tears
to buy me back from what,
not knowing what else to name it,
I call "immunity from my own happiness".

My optimism just gave me a hard push,
my cry just threw me out of my own rage.
Unable to find which word best suits
the end of a silence that never wanted to remain silent,
I start to feel that I am sought by the one miracle
my self-confidence is hiding behind my enthusiasm.

I'm not satisfied with just becoming again
the gorgeous gladiator of my cowardice,
I want to be my heart's most humble treasure,
the one thing inside her she will never wish to surrender
to the rewards my next victory
has been demanding from her for some time now
to let me make her mine.
For years now I've owed my life a big apology.
Today I will find the courage to beg her forgiveness.

Since then I tread on the anguish of a conscience
that's forced every morning to adapt my lies
to the shape of the new truth I use,
a truth that I am not sure anymore is mine.

All these years I've been praising my words,
now the time has come to become their loyal employee.
Now I don't even trust my silence
with all that I cannot say anymore.

The cunning little devil, to protect herself from my own stupidity,
leaves me alone, absolutely free to paint for hours
on the words I will never utter
the indestructible memories of those moments
when I surrendered without receiving anything for it
my next breath to my biggest discontent.

It is her that doesn't stop urging me
to start taking again those endless solitary walks
on the most uncompromising part of my self-confidence,
the part that buys my future from any part of my past
my happiness never found any use for.
Thus my life learned from an early age
to endlessly paint herself with those unscrupulous pitch-black stains
that were quick to appear on my soul's body
every time she heard my logic cheering her wildly.

My most ambitious feelings of guilt are so relieved
when they finally manage, after being drenched for many hours in sadness,
to inherit the burdens of my most emotionally dishonest cry
which no longer knows itself what it's screaming about.
Impressed by the ingenuity of my wickedness
and unable to understand what the more than ten fingerprints
that my words leave on her want to confide to her,
she refuses to believe in the deafening whisper
uttered by my melancholy when with sheer joy
she manages to convince me to once more become
the eternal slave of the part of my own charisma
that never managed to charm me.

Without aiming to, I've managed to become the happy waiter of my own mediocrity,
a pitiful but extremely effective porter of those secret spots inside me
which I'm trying tooth and nail to never learn how to locate
because then I will be forced to acknowledge their existence.

I tumbled for hours arm in arm with the pain
felt by all those words in my life
I did my best to hate as quickly as I could
before making an effort to realize how much I truly need them.

whether it was trying to hug me or drown me.
After a few agonizing moments
I began to feel that this liquid was none other
than what my own sweat always wanted to be.

I felt as if, instead of the highly competent lie of an ulterior motive
which my logic always used so well to convince me
to do something I was not sure I wanted to do,
the honesty of every brave battle I fought
for the first time in my life ran after me to hug me.

My soul began timidly to trust again the bill
my hope has been sending her all these years
at the end of every miserable period of my life.
The next step suddenly doesn't seem as steep as before.
The newborn hope won't anxiously search, the minute she's born,
to find the remnants of charity
that the justification of who I've become
has quietly tucked away inside her.

Suddenly under this blinding light
which total darkness knows so well how to hide close to its very own end,
I sense, without being able to see it clearly,
the smallest truth that lives in my conscience
bending over my lies and very gently forgiving them one by one.
Meanwhile, my insatiable past refuses to trust its own demands any longer
and leaves upset to go as quickly as possible
to lock itself up in a sorrow from way back,
one of the very few sorrows of mine it still trusts blindly.

Liberated from the expectations my past has for me
I asked for the minimum silence that usually hides itself
in the interpretation of every emotion of mine
I would like to start trusting in the future
before I even begin feeling it.

I clothed my heart in the colors of the first smile
I saw on my face wishing to dominate my sadness
and immediately started shredding the flavor my next day wants to have
so that I will be able to lean, to rest
on the breathless affection of those emotions
my logic is urging me not to feel.
Life of mine, be patient,
my next sorrow just handed in her resignation.

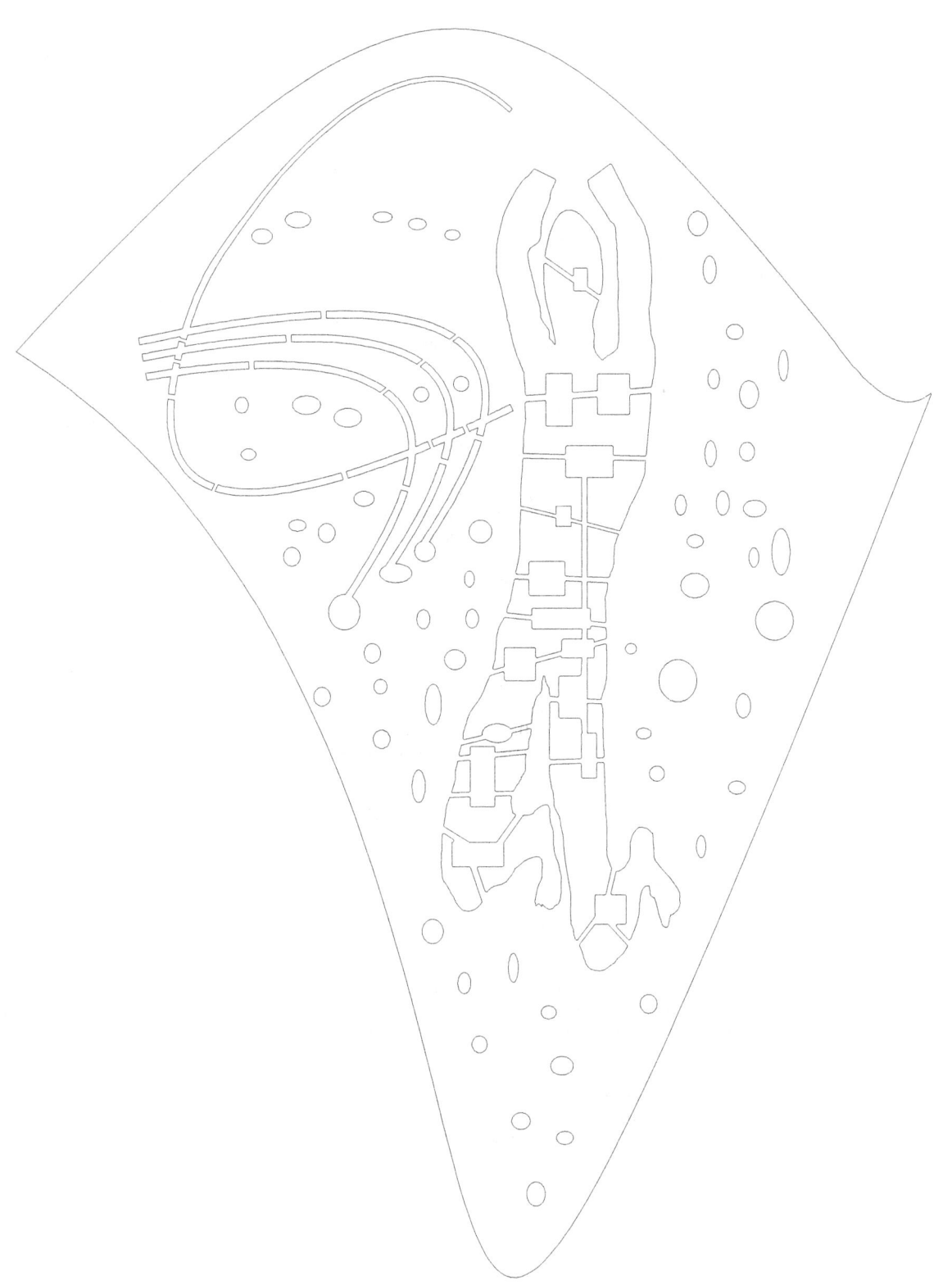

He is alone, just him and the miserable absence of his own truth
that does not know anymore
how to make him even more unhappy that he already is.
To get away from her, he tries with a sleight of hand move
to fit perfectly into the storm he just gave birth to
which, the more time goes by and it realizes how weak its father is,
the more it wants to devour him.

He is exposed to the omnipotence of his own weaknesses.
Facing the storm that never wanted to define its own beginning
but always knew what its end would be like,
he falls on the condescending ground his life treads on daily
and begins to regret everything
his logic didn't let him learn how to dream.
Suspended at the edge of his greatest fear
he is ready to fight for the white that dares to live inside him
before he's forced to concede that his personal winter,
a winter that only he can feel in the middle of August,
will manage by the end of the day
to enwrap him in its velvety black.

Squeezing as many cries as he could
into the first silence that wanted to talk to him,
he pulled down the zipper of his optimism
and crammed as many sunbeams as he could into his body,
which had already started falling to its knees well before he did.

He donned that rock-hard image of his
which he found in his soul's deepest drawer
and, already defeated by the one fear of his he could never befriend,
he awaits the orders of his own apologies
to attack the latest model of his cowardice.

Embraced by his entire body, except his own hands,
he stands alone in an incredibly ambitious, drenching rain,
a rain made of bright red silences,
in which he has been hiding every time in his life he refused to feel
before he tried to understand what he had already begun to think,
and of deep blue silences,
in which he has been hiding the shy apology
he owes to each new day that believed in him
without being influenced by what the previous one
kept on shouting at it.

He spread his palms as wide as he could,
almost uprooting them from his own hands,
so that he could try to catch this rain to the last drop.
He wanted so much to be able to craft without anyone's help
a shiny sword out of all the precious drops
that fell with otherworldly force
on the surface of his own beliefs.

For the first time in his life he found the courage
to take all his clothes off,
plunge into the darkest part of his greatest fear

which were so painstakingly made for me
by the part of my mind that still prefers to be ruthless rather than innocent.

In the end it seems to me that I want much more than I think
to become one with any piece of my intellect
that's resting at the edge of my luck,
waiting for her to begin translating to it
the genuineness of that glance my future gave me years ago,
the one which believed in my malice
more than it ever believed in me.

I convinced my life to deliberately start making spelling mistakes
so I can try to save my soul from my intelligence's uncompromising vanity.
Injustice will die the moment it gets touched
by the first sunbeam of courage which just realized
that midnight gave it as a present last night an adolescent darkness
which I know will refuse to listen to what my intelligence has to say
unless it first speaks with my soul.

For years now I've stopped underestimating the power
borne by the post-midnight rewards
offered to me by the guilt that permanently lives a sunshine away from me.
They want so much to make me betray the first attempt by the morning sun
to convince me to hide my pessimism
in the little silver box the moon gave me last night as a gift.
How much I fear those moments of my life
when loneliness begins to manufacture her own silence
and logic her own cheapness!

The insatiable fog, which the reign of my insecurities
ceaselessly keeps on churning out from within it,
has the unique ability to instantly fall in love
with what it cannot fit in the embrace of its deepest gray.
Feeling totally harmless, I lie down
looking into the eyes of yet another night
whose many wounds, most of which I had inflicted on it before it was even born,
I haven't stopped tending to,
hearing the self-adjusting sense of fairness
which I would like to believe I still possess
shout from deep inside me:
"Come, grab my hand and together let's become what we fear".

before they start trampling their own future.

Will you come with me to help me apologize
to the stair steps of my life I no longer have the courage to climb?
The perfume a lie of mine uses
to hide me from my self-awareness.
I raised my head, looked at the part of the sky that seemed emptier
and saw thousands of crimson questions
hanging from every sunshine that belonged to me. Why?

Testing the appropriate technique for letting my conscience
make an emergency landing in reality.
The day that man will be disappointed
by all the material goods his own lies bring him.
This happens when a mind's future
is different from that of its owner.

Why did you let your ego during the rest of the day
decorate you with its most beautiful delusions?
It's not time yet for you to try to find out how much your compassion is worth
in your happiness' exchange.
It might be time, though, for you to cut in half
the infinity that has surrounded you from all the secret corners of your sorrow
so you can find out where this cheerful emotion
you surrendered tied hand and foot to your melancholy
springs forth from.

Stop burying the oxygen you breathe in the ground
so you won't be able to ever use it again.
When the wind tries to find a way to chase off me
the smell of my next mistake.
What I learned about you while collecting the crumbs of the echo
left by your insecurities on top of the table while we were fighting.

Come back, come along with those old used fogs of yours
to teach me how to reveal myself to those parts of my future
I don't know how to hide from my insecurities.
Catharsis doesn't have any other means of transit
to help me get across to my soul
without getting dirty by touching my honesty.
Today muddy silences are arguing with squeaky clean truths.

A look made of sleepy words and expendable consciences.
A look made of words that cannot stand
expressing what their owner wants any longer.
A look made of words that don't want to speak anymore
because they no longer know how to be quiet.

The exact spot in my mind where I put all the resignation letters
my reality sent me at any given time.
Say what you want to tell me before I finish repairing my normality
from the punches your imagination threw at it.
This is why two people, the moment they decide to stay together,
immediately start making a common abyss
in which they will throw any part of themselves
they never understood how it works.

Just one smile of yours can paint on my soul
the finish line of my sorrow.

What less am I, I wonder, than the director my happiness chose
to show the people I love all that it could not understand?
In victory you first realize where your darkness starts
before you start distinguishing amid your ungrateful glow
the spot of your self-reliance where your own light chose to fade out.
In defeat you realize the limits of your pessimism.
That's why when I lose I will finally manage to figure out
what my victories were whispering to my dreams all this time.

To get to know you, I had to first get to know myself.
To get to know you, I had, while I was anxiously running back and forth
right outside the look your soul gave me,
to go past my embarrassment
-which was running a few inches ahead of my most unbearable misgivings,
until I inadvertently stumbled on an enthusiasm of mine
I had not seen since my adolescence.
To be quite honest, I didn't even know
that it still lived in me after all these years.
Maybe because the sneaky devil had managed to get born
seconds before I was.
How I'd love to live a life in which my next joy is produced
by what I feel and not what I understand!

I came before you and extending my left arm
I left in the middle of your palm the bit of sunshine
my very hopes had earlier grabbed from inside my own future.
My poor soul held it in her hand for three days
not knowing what to do with it.

Will I ever be able to figure out, I wonder, how the hell the dawn
already managed to forget the secrets
the loose-lipped night revealed to it a few hours ago?
Exasperated by my inability to come up with an answer,
I rushed to hide in my whisper all those words
entrusted to me by those deep red, misspelled fogs
which I was watching all night coming from afar
to help me hide me from myself.
These are the fogs that, as soon as they enter one's soul,
instantly start placing one shortcoming of his under another,
building these very clever downhills
that have discovered how to be so slippery by adjusting their slope in such a way
that they manage to bring down even the most balanced person
who might try to cross them.

I'll confess something to you.
When years ago I heard your voice for the first time
I immediately closed my eyes,
and plunged with all the speed I could gather into that word of yours
which during our first date you did all you could not to utter,
the one you had made out of the softest emotional silk
I had ever touched in my life.

I wanted to have time to grasp it as gently as I could
and spread it all over my wounds
to let it free to figure out what they are made of
and in so doing make them feel me, maybe even understand me.
I wanted to do that before the friction of the air around me
made it more ordinary, less pure,
less recruited by the excess toughness
I have forced the people around me to possess
to be able to withstand living with me.

I'll confess something else to you.
I found you in the part of my soul
which I thought I had lost access to years ago.
I found you in the question
which for years now I believed my self-confidence
would never answer for me.

won't stop constantly patrolling
around the most unguarded edges of our hearts.
It is always ready to remind every emotion it sees passing by
that every beautiful memory our two hearts have produced together
is forced to live in the hopelessly cowardly private cell
which our two minds gave us as a gift
at the end of the first day we met.

Why does an old photo need to be a reminder of who you are not today?
That dam frame is so adept at wrestling with our marriage,
by simultaneously using all four of its stifling corners,
trimming here and pushing there
till it manages to fit everything we are inside its own body
which the rules of our life have so carefully constructed.
What else is a picture frame anyway than a cell
where those emotions that no longer want to feel
are relegated to live forever?

How similar are ultimately picture frames to our very life!
Logic sits outside safeguarding the soul
she keeps imprisoned in the body
so she won't liberate herself and rush into the outside world
proclaiming to all her very expensive truths.

Ever since I decided to become my most transparent miracle
I began to study my courage from the beginning.
It was then when, forgetting where I wanted to go
I began to slowly realize that before starting to walk forward
I first had to learn how to properly walk backwards.

I feel that I owe my life before reaching its end to revisit its start.
With me I will take those questions
that my beginning always wanted to ask me,
the ones that always managed to find an extremely simple way
to slip in whenever they wanted through my cowardice's armor
hoping to discover what material it is made of.

They want so much to surge back inside me
to find out what makes me every morning five minutes before I wake myself up
wake up my ulterior motive and try to convince it,
without anyone overhearing, to go work for me for yet another day.
I want so much to make it bring back to me
the questions my ambiguity ordered from it
in those hours of my life that have secured immunity from my logic.

and immunities out of brand new guilt
so that it would run over my future
and make it disappear from my self-esteem's field of vision.

Then again it might be what is left of him
when the ambition of his sorrow
decides to leave him alone, even if only for a short while.
While hearing the warm applause of my biggest shortcoming
I start watching the grand parade
of the most defective abyss that lives in me
pass through my last truth,
the one I don't know how to defend from the attacks of my silence.
Please tell me these are not the boundaries of my soul
with her next triumph!

I feel so good now that the memory of my meanness is almost full!
I felt so good when in the love
with which your shiest embrace wrapped me
I discovered how many different kinds of desert I hid inside me!
Please, help me.
Teach me how to hold in my hands my sweetest word
without tainting it.
Teach me how to grasp in my hands whichever part of my character
I was unable to talk to even once in my life
without ending up offending it.

What makes me believe that I will be able to see the entire expanse of the sky
that will pass over me today?
I don't know if the sunset
will later want to belong entirely to the part of the sky
my pessimism hasn't let me see for days now.
I don't know if the sky today
will let the sunset spread its colors like a playful painter
on any part of his he wants
just to try to create thousands of minor miracles,
miracles he will freely offer to every soul that is watching.

For some reason I can't figure out
the sky today needs order more than it needs beauty.
So I am left alone hanging out with what's left
of the frantic heavenly dance of red and gold,
unable to understand what they want to create exclusively for me
in the back side of my soul.
Now I am certain. Any miracle man has ever performed was born at the place
where the end of his soul borders with the beginning of his own imagination.

I'm left speechless watching the remotest parts of the sunset
carefully taking in their hands one by one my most precious emotions
and placing them at the spots in my soul that are deeper than my sorrow.
These are the spots that not even she wants to touch
before she finds a way to ensure that she'll be able to locate them again
so that she can give them back to it.

helping us this way to forget, even for just a few minutes,
the ambition of the slightest vanity each one's sorrow contained.
Who knows, maybe this way we hoped that we would manage to find out
how high our happiness could reach
before it started tearing into a thousand pieces
all the blue that the sky did not want to have in it at that moment.

It was the first time that my heart, no matter how hard she tried,
could not explain to me where her limits ended
and where the limits of yours began.
It was the first time I felt the body of the person I love,
without even moving, catch one by one the toxic words
my mind hurled on the fight's table
and toss them in the trash.
It really wanted me to hear all that which my good qualities
avoided telling me for quite some time now.

From your embrace I learned how not to hate,
how not to envy anything I can no longer fit in mine.
I learned how to touch any part of my soul that,
since it can't defeat my sorrow anymore,
has run off to hide inside her.
Embrace of mine, will you please teach me
how to stay silent without offending,
how to touch something without demanding to conquer it?
Greed of mine, will you teach me how to bend as much as I can
over the bottomless well I host in the center of my life
in which I keep the treasure of my own soul
without being in danger of falling in?

so that my adolescence won't ever be able to prove to me
who I told her that I would someday become?
So here's how the part of my mind that on a daily basis
I leave deliberately ambiguous can have the opportunity to embrace me
without ever having to touch me.
Here's how one of my favorite qualms can survive for years
away from the most fascinating dreams
my feelings of guilt are dreaming on its behalf.
Hesitantly unraveling one by one the questions
my day had already started asking me
even though it's still only six forty five am,
I decided today to try to become the faceless burglar of our common shadow,
the one our bodies jointly start building from scratch
every time they want to hide us in the back side of our sorrow,
before I'm forced to become its sole owner.

Perhaps then I might be able to understand
why in every relationship I started in my life
the moment I looked into the eyes of my partner for the first time
I felt as if our two bodies, without knowing if they were trying to wrestle or make love,
started casting anew a common shadow
even if there was no light around us at the time to give birth to it.
It took me a long time to realize
that the darkness that knows how to survive around a couple
becomes much smarter than both of them as time goes by.
It knows how to hide within it words that should never be spoken,
how to reveal expressions that neither of them had the courage
to let free to say what each of them felt,
how to draw out of their mouths words that were born eternally silent,
how to instantly hide under awkward moments
controversial answers whose time had not come yet
to reveal the material they were made of.
Ah, what happens in one's life
when heretical darknesses and blasphemous silences conspire…

I wonder what would I understand
if I could sit right in the middle of our common sorrow,
spread my arms as wide as I could
and embraced all the darkness that can still stand to live around us?
Would I find out how much my own brightness pains me?
I highly doubt it.
Would I find out how many questions
the first sunbeam that will shine on two bodies
that just finished making love for the first time wants to ask?
Probably as many as it needs to liberate us from our own shadows
since it's this sunbeam that later won't allow us to figure out
which part of our character it deliberately avoids illuminating
so that we won't be able to realize its terrifying dimensions.

without simultaneously forcing his soul to become smaller.

What can I say? As far as I can remember, I was almost always able
to quickly find inside me one of those miraculous "maybes"
that was willing to go sit between me and my partner
during those times in my life when the emotional stress I felt
was greater than my emotional intelligence.
To get away from the rage my own mind felt for me
I pushed away from me everyone and everything,
even the most precious parts of my life,
and after searching as best I could
through all the souls of the people I loved in the past one by one,
I pounced like a rabid dog to invade the first soul
that was inadvertently left unlocked by her owner.

Doing all I could to avoid entering
my next dignity ahead of my pessimism,
I fought tooth and nail to fit
as big a part of my self-confidence as I could
into the only two hues of my soul
that were willing at the time
to help me paint my future using no colors, just the edges of shadows.

Could it be inside the dreams that my arrogance dreams on my behalf
every time when, annoyed with her,
I push her away from me towards the end of my truth?
I don't know.

By using all my powers of persuasion,
I tried to sell the mistakes made by those self- indulgent theories of life
that live constantly lying next to my sofa's most charming lie
to the passion of my sweat, but I failed.
I tried to match the thoughts of my comfort
with the hopes of my optimism, but I failed.
I am left alone, standing awkwardly in the middle of my most ineffective laziness
trying to find a way to chase after those hopes
with the checkbook which the courage of my greatest inadequacy
puts in my right hand every morning just after I get out of bed.

Since then I've been sharing the priorities of my boredom
with whatever my courage asks of my next decision.
When I go to sleep every night
I stick my face for a few moments on the questions my pillow has
while observing a few inches away from the one finger of mine
which believes that it can reach further than any other
my enthusiasm struggling desperately in the twilight
to locate its only customer.
It is the moment when the cold, totally unemotional truth of convenience,
the one that ignored me for so long,
starts speaking to me again to tell me things my lies have confided to it,
secrets that nobody else could possibly know.

In the emotionally very expensive gray of this image
I relearn how to properly count my fears from scratch
without omitting anyone I don't know by name,
while I keep on searching for those sunbeams left on the floor of my mind
by all that I had the courage to hope for yesterday.
My ambiguity, without wasting any time,
asked me to pick a fight with my self-indulgence
and I, before agreeing with it to fall much lower,
will first have to realize how low I have already fallen.

In the afternoon's deep orange heavily-armed despair,
which won't lend me even a single minute
out of its middle-aged, slightly tired strength,
I end up seeing the dangerously steep downhill right before me
wink at me playfully as it tries the shape of its steepness on my body.
What made me believe that I have only one truth to spare in my life?

don't help me develop my strengths the way you want
so that I'm able to get back into my life again
through the back side of my own splendor.

How can a man find a way
to stop the civil war between his own emotions
without betraying that part of his soul
for which he's more proud than any other?
I knew that I wouldn't easily find the answer
so I sat for a while a few feet away from myself
staring at my vanity admiring the trophies
it won on my behalf.
A bit later I began to unfurl from within my soul
the deepest affection I have in me
and started throwing it on any emotion of mine I found before me
to which I couldn't explain what my shortcomings want from me,
I couldn't explain how much each shortcoming of mine hurts me
every time it tries to do something good for me.

I turn my gaze towards the darkest point in my life
and place the word I can no longer keep inside me
in the only part of my mouth where I can't taste its flavor anymore.
I see three threadbare thoughts
sitting fearfully next to each other at the edge of my mind
waiting for my insecurity to choose
which one it will throw again into the spot of my mouth
where darkness can no longer bear to live
and so ends up kicking out any words that try to hide in it.

Restless, I have straddled the hands of my clock
and I'm rotating around time's carefree awkwardness
hearing with every beat of my heart
my boredom measuring how much courage is still left inside me.
It wants so much to make me figure out
if it's me who shields the next happy moment in my life from my misery
or the other way around.

Looking awkwardly at myself in that mirror
which by itself has managed to find a way to move
from the center of my room to the center of my life,
I realize that I am tightly wedged
in between two simultaneous reflections of it.

or the worse enemy of a vanity
that no longer knows how to remain private.

I stand bewildered, completely abandoned
by the image I would like to display in the mirror,
watching the two reflections fight
over which one will manage to hide in time
what it ought to show me.
Panicked, I start looking to find the first darkness
which with a single merciful move
would free me from this unbearable torment.
I feel my words run like mad up and down my body
trying to find another way to get out besides my mouth.
So I begin to run myself until I stop some time later
in front of the most unspoiled, virgin darkness I have seen in my life.
There with the help of the part of my imagination
that always considers a half-finished lie
better than a half-ruined truth,
I see the finish line of my joy
flirt with the first moment of my next misery.

Unable to cope emotionally
with the significance of what I was experiencing at the time,
my tears started wrestling with their own past
hoping they might manage to explain
their meaning to my meaning,
their future to my future.
They didn't succeed.
The trash tears leave behind
every time they triumphantly parade before mother sorrow
was clearer than any other emotion I could feel right then.
I have the impression that this must be the side of my weakness
that has stolen me from my future.
Then again it might be that version of my sorrow
which lately has been protecting me
from any moment in my life I try to find a way
to feel more real than human.

I don't know how I found myself praying on my knees
in what in the beginning seemed to me to be the least emotionally flat edge
of a field whose soil instead of grains of earth
was composed of millions of blue silences.
It was the field that instead of trees had in it half finished thoughts
in hundreds of colors except red,
thoughts whose trunks rose
up to thirty feet above the ground.

In a spot a bit left of its midpoint
I sat next to a half-buried piece of steel
which, ignoring anything happening around it, was standing almost upright,
proud, but at the same time enslaved by its total lack of freedom.
It was absolutely sure of itself.
It was equally sure of its future.
It felt all powerful because it had managed to hide in the safest spot within it
the promises of the one who once assured it
that whatever happened, he would look after it daily for the rest of its life.

Having nothing better to do
and having spent my gaze till then
looking at everything else around me,
I let my idle curiosity scrutinize it on my behalf.
I sat at that spot for quite some time,
while it paid me little notice,
although once in a while our awkward glances would cross each other
the same way you look at a fellow traveler on a train,
not because you want to observe him
but because you've grown tired of observing the person next to him.
It's a strange moment when someone
orders his eyes to stop seeing on behalf of his mind
and start wrestling with his own awkwardness
over who will first defeat his next minute.
Even stranger is the moment when he decides to go across
and reach the end of his eyes
to get to where his soul starts distinguishing what she sees.

After a while I found the courage to go near that piece of steel,
bent down, fell to my knees and began to hear coming from inside it
a bizarre sound, something like a whisper, like a lament.
This sound welled up at regular intervals
from the rust that had enwrapped its body so tenderly all these years
to protect it from the indifference contained
in the thousands of glances people gave it from time to time.

which was long abandoned by its owner in the back side of time.

While it was telling me what it went through in its life
I felt my gaze grab my hand and lay it gently on its surface
to touch, to figure out from what material,
what kind of wounds the actual rust covering it was made of.
Meanwhile, while we were talking, the poor rust tried in vain
to wrap everything I heard in a different kind of truth
than the one the piece of steel was telling me about.

A few minutes later I began to discover that over the entire length of its body
it had incredibly deep scratches, almost human-like scars,
like those dug by the plow of time
on the skin of a person who every day that goes by
is forced to follow in chains the promises time has made him
in whichever part of reality it wants to take him.
It seems that it's not only man who has the capacity
to hide so much weakness in his own strength.

The more I kept touching it
the more I felt that its rust was starting to feel more comfortable with me
and not only stopped trying to run away from me,
but began to caress me back.
I felt as if I heard an incredibly white silence well up from inside it,
or was it my own heart that couldn't draw from inside her
a single meaningful word to speak with?
I really love those astonishing silences
which, not having said a single word,
have already managed to tell the whole truth!
I heard a call for help coming from its depths
dressed in the simplest, most common phrase
as if such a solid material, one of the most time-resistant in the world
was ashamed to show how weak it actually feels
to someone, who until a few minutes ago, was a complete stranger.

As time went by its caress started slowly piercing
from end to end the absolute silence around us
producing from within it a sound resembling something like a song
that wasn't content with just being a sequence of notes
but demanded to be the narrative of a truth,
or even a lament of it that wanted first to touch the injury itself
to feel what its pain means
before it starts singing about it.

I wonder, if such a durable material
after many years of neglect
has reached a point of hurting so much
that it ends up feeling weaker than it actually is,
what happens to a human heart like mine
which isn't made out of steel
but out of ordinary lies that no longer know how to speak to my future
about who they would want to have me be
and out of stunning truths that no longer know
how to defend who I already am?

Searching inside me to find out why I cannot answer
the questions my coldness asks me
without asking my compassion for help,
I realize that I cannot answer them
without forcing them to start giving birth from within them
to other tougher, more ruthless questions.
So that's why, knowing that nothing rusts faster than lies,
I wrapped myself in its rust, I wrapped him in my own rust,
and let my delusions besiege my future
conquering on my behalf
all that I will never manage to conquer myself…

I feel compelled to carry along with me through the night
to any part of my own imagination my dreams want to take me.

I am tired of not daring.
I am tired of not daring to feel.
I am tired of not daring to feel all those emotions
that have already felt me.

About a half-finished stupidity further on,
the weight of my next decision
refuses to sit with me any longer
and upset gets up and leaves.

My indecisiveness once again got her legs entangled
in the questions my courage does not want to ask me.
It begins resolutely to write on my forehead
with some incredibly intense thick yellow-green letters
all that I fear more than anything else to feel.
I remain on my knees trying to figure out
the new vocabulary my hesitations want to use
to describe to me what the most uncharted part of my courage wants me to do
before I'm forced to get up and take the first step inside it.

I'm afraid to feel what I already know.
I'm afraid to throw away what I have already forgotten.
I'm not afraid, however, to introduce myself again to all that has already forgotten me.
A few silken seconds beyond the spot where my body is lying
I notice the sunset speaking softly with midnight.
I don't know, but somehow I think they're talking about me.

As time goes by I keep on hearing my reality confiding its worst fears
to those of my virtues that still speak to me.
My kisses chase after me to convince me
that the time has come for me to try to understand
what it is that I want them to do for me.
Meanwhile, the questions that my malice has
try to persuade me that, no matter how many years I live,
I'll never need to try to answer them.

Once again I failed to touch my humanity
before I accidentally fell on it.
Once again I failed to hear what my beliefs had been shouting at me for hours now.
My soul, though, managed to take an oath
to never again offend the rags I make her wear
and I, moved by her decision, immediately embraced the kind of happiness
in which a laughter that does not ever want to end
is searching inside it for the momentary sorrow
that will help it explain the purpose of its own existence.

I am left alone, proud to still be standing,
proud to still be able to walk using legs
which are immersed one in the velvet whisper of my own loneliness
and the other in the granite echo of my own dreams.
I'm doing everything I can
to traverse the half-demolished darknesses
whose blackness I managed to defeat a short while ago for the first time.
Only overweight self-confidences fit to go
through small keyholes.

I will become again the decommissioned interpreter
of those five minutes before the orgasm of my cowardice
that don't seem to want to stop living permanently inside me.
Where the hell was I hiding those invisible heartbeats of mine
which always had the courage to fight against
those times in my life when I wanted to feel pain more than feel love,
the moments when I was quick to betray myself
rather than willing to defend him.

I locked myself for hours in these moments,
the moments of one's life that demand to look more like eternal apathy
rather than the bits of velvet enthusiasm they actually are.
They are so smart!
They know how to follow the orders, without seeming to obey,
coming from the scrupulous dust of my life made of those light blue darknesses
which always knew how to cover up with its sleight-of-hand moves
every disadvantage of mine that was more ambitious than any other
without appearing to be trying to help me.

I feel like, before I even finish thinking them up,
my own words will instantly turn their back on my mouth
and attack it to make me bleed, to make me suffer.
Shaken, I rush to collect from the least illuminated corners of my mind
the part of my kindness I found discarded on its floor
so as not to give my delusions the chance
to ask me to lend them as much cowardice as they'll still need
so that they may continue attacking you.

I kissed as quickly as I could
the first minute of my life that hesitated to spit on my face,
stole as much extra affection as I could
from the first word that refused to fight with the people I love,
and, slipping between those emotions
the twilight that always belonged to my melancholy is getting ready to give birth to,
found the courage to ask my mind
if it's willing to let me become even for a short while
the man who fears his own wings
less than his own weight.

I am in a hurry to persuade myself to forget how to understand what I am seeing
hoping its feeble glow will have time to hide behind the horizon
so it won't get a chance to shed light
on the greedy desires my guilt continues to have
and force me to realize how many they are.

In which of my pockets did I hide the start of the laughter
I've wanted to become myself for so long now?
The poor thing's eyes filled with tears when it found out
that I began just a few minutes ago to dig in the deepest spots inside me
solely to find the proof that this laughter never belonged to me, was never mine!

Every mind lives in the mire
made of those thoughts it never managed to produce.
So does mine.
It seems that I finally found the courage to ask my compassion
to not give me what I want to take from it,
persuading my mind to get unstuck from this mire
and my feet from the tracks made for them by the smile I used as fuel
to reach the front door of my optimism.

My dream has already convinced me to forget it behind tonight.
It does all it can to make me not take with me
any part of tomorrow is not to its advantage to remember.
So I broke in two that strange recyclable blue pain
I had not yet found a way to figure out why I felt it,
took its most painful part and kissed it on the spot
that wanted to make me hurt the most,
welcomed to my body the brand new steps
my ego ordered from that reality of my life
which it considers more convenient for it to live in,
sang my fears until they started to amuse me
–maybe until they began to fear me less,
tore into a thousand pieces the miserable wallet
in which my arrogance puts those currency notes of hers
each one of which separately promised me
that it will never want to talk again to any other,
and anxiously ran to the front door of the coming day
to see what my past had already left for me there.

Is there a longer journey for someone I wonder
than the quest to find himself in what he already is?
Exhausted after so many hours
of searching in the weakest part of my heart
to find the strongest emotion I can feel,
I lifted all the sunrise I could fit in my palms
and wrapped it around that side of my heart
which until recently I thought its only use was to act as my emotional armor.

I clenched in my hand the least false lie I had in my head right then
and ran to get out of whichever emotion in my life I have left unfinished,
whichever emotion of mine I have offended in the past
by not daring to feel it all to its end,
hoping this way it might allow me to meet for the first time what I already know.
How do you introduce yourself to someone you already know?
By letting your soul get to know him the second time around
moments before your logic asks him the first question.

Only my injuries now have the right to dream
the best teenage dreams I never had time to see
because my adolescence was in a hurry to end
before I managed to realize which parts of me
I asked it to never surrender to my adulthood
before I found a way to protect them from my happiness.

Why is the trashcan the most honest spot in a house?
Perhaps because when a man sits for a while across from a blank page he often tears it because
he knows that since he won't manage to write anything of value on it,
it will soon start writing on him itself.
Are there, I wonder, cleaner emotional spots than sewers on the earth?
I very much doubt it, because sewers have nothing to hide.

Will you please stop tormenting me
by forcing me to live a silence away from my most favorite word?
Though unable to figure out why,
I feel like I just took part
in the last military coup my serenity had in her.
Watching my malice's defeat
lose somewhere inside me the part of her beginning which she hated,
I urged your most misspelled erotic caresses
to try to find in the less sensitive parts of my character
the reason they try so hard to make me not want to understand what I feel
every time you disappear from my side and leave me alone with my frigidity.

How I suffer every time I cannot figure out
whether the shadow I see before me
each time I let the meaning of my life illuminate me anyway it wants
is that of my body or my soul.
I really wish I could explain the reason why for the first time today
an old shadow of my body whose requests I never managed to satisfy
chose to come back to visit with me.
It's not accidental. It cannot be accidental!

The damn shadow has such an abundance of silent darkness inside it
to cast over the world around it
that it makes the least important glance I ever had at the disposal of my eyes
plead with me to let it leave my side
so I won't force it any more to touch whatever I can no longer reach,
not even by using my most cunning thought.
I feel so strange when I realize that the least important glance I have in me
can, if it wishes, see even further than my own imagination.
What freedom and yet what a limitation!

who no longer remembers how to translate every minute of his life
into a language his emotions can understand.
This is the gratitude a pain feels
toward the very person who chose to defeat his emotions
by simply tossing them back into his past one by one
instead of admitting that they are entirely his own.

I forced the sorrow that every phobia of mine feels
to apologize to all that I gain by losing.
Now I am certain.
I have a soul that no longer knows how to balance on her balance,
doesn't even know how to persuade my logic
to listen to what she doesn't want to tell her.

Thus dwindles the amount of that invisible dust
my optimism convinces tomorrow to buy from it every midnight.
It's the dust that it will soon use to cover
any part of my character it won't be able to understand.
So I end up falling asleep a little later than I had figured,
arm in arm with my guilt,
which I was able to convince today
for the first time in years to talk to me again.

By morning I should have finished counting
all the compensation I have to offer my time
so it will let me go through that door
which has been standing for hours seven feet behind my back
and enter the part of tomorrow
that believes that by passing through it
I'll become better than the person I was yesterday.

My most ambitious thoughts began to tie the moment hand and foot
and are now ready to toss it into the landfill
where the sky's great compassion
dumps all the "I can'ts" I have uttered,
the ones it already failed from passing the grade
because it figured out exactly what I meant to say.
Hearing my past going out of breath
while searching like mad to find out how much strength I still hide in me,
I climbed on the shoulders of my courage
to feel even for a few seconds like half a winner.

Today I hope to avoid
being trampled by the back side of my life,
which unfortunately can still run much faster than me.

because it wanted to have the right to determine them on its own.
Same thing for my soul.
She always used to grab whichever emotion of mine
didn't know what to feel at the time
and with it carve out her path in any part of my reality she chose.
Once she was finished, she always released it in the middle of my ambiguity
for my enthusiasm to come and take it by the hand
so they could run together to any point in my life it wanted.

Today this torrent chooses to spring forth
where my self-awareness borders with the most insignificant future
I will let my self-preservation choose for me,
a future which I'm almost certain
that by now wants to resemble me as little as possible.
As the years went by I eventually completed its containment
so it won't surprise either me, or the people around me.
This way I managed to tame the river
because I was able to forget how to value all the good it could carry in it,
because I managed to hate the reason it existed.
So I ended up subjugating it to the will of my guilt,
those ambitious mumblings of my logic.

Whatever man doesn't know how to love with his soul
he instantly makes his logic devise new ways to hate it.
He really feels such a need to defeat it
because when he knows that he cannot win,
to be able to survive in the same mind as his ego,
he must immediately start tearing down the reason he competed in the first place.
Life despises all the embezzled ambiguities that were born victories
and adores all the defeats that were born draws.
Maybe this way she manages to not fall in love with what she always wanted to be
before she crawls to what she actually is
and asks it to let her live with it.

I didn't know how to make any emotion I felt
believe that it was a product of my honesty,
because I didn't know how to convince myself
to not feel ashamed for my bankrupt imperfections.
I didn't know how not to bow my head
each time what I felt passed before my logic
to get her consent so that it could exit my mouth
to try to explain to the people I love who I really am.
For years I didn't stop day or night building on the river of my soul
impregnable dams here, high walls there,
making its flow perfectly controlled, calm, predictable, acquiescent.
Thus I deadened my soul.
Thus I deadened my life.
Here's how you can kill yourself

what I always thought was my treasured serenity.
They are the ones who left their lazy descendants
to daily take care of what's left of my imagination
just after I gave it as a gift an additional amount of normality
apart from what it already had in it.

One for you and one for the sadness that will come find me when you leave.
How I would love to have the ability whenever I want
to let my passion pour out of my soul
so it can rush as fast as it can
to embrace anyone walking by me
until it makes him seem more like
who he himself would like to be.

Who knows? Do you think I will ever understand
why the bankrupt promises I made my heart
every time I could stand to look yours in the eyes
without fearing all that I won't be able to feel,
came to take me by the hand to where the road
won't recognize the spot where it ends
because it is afraid that, by doing so,
it will be forced to identify the spot from where it started?

For hours now my passion is doing all it can to protect me
from the mistakes which in its opinion I am forced to make
by that side of my self-esteem that doesn't care if I'm happy
as long as each day I take another step closer
to becoming the man I am told I should be.
I can no longer stand to watch my ego
whenever it sees me leave the hideout
my loneliness has dug for me to hide me from my own happiness
rush to hang a huge pink sign on my chest that reads:
"I am the back side of my success."

My enthusiasm is about to plunge between me and my tranquility
unable to understand why I feel compelled
to keep on defeating my character strengths
each time my compassion runs after me
trying to tie a blindfold over my eyes
so that I won't be able to watch to the end
my duel with any part of my happiness I haven't killed yet.

Seeing the battle progressing,
my damn normality quickly went and sat
between my heart and me.
Stretching its shadow as far as it can
it will attempt to not let me see
even a single square inch of any part inside me
that refuses to follow the part of my logic
which from the moment it was born
believed more in the emotional profit of a dollar bill
than in the compassion of a smile.

I pretended to urge it to carry out of my body
any emotion my soul didn't know how to feel
letting as usual my self-preservation like the good traffic cop it is
maintain total control over which emotion heads to the outside world
and which stays forever inside me.
There, just outside my mind's customs office,
with the help of those worldviews I always used
to leave outside any visiting thoughts I deemed undesirable,
I managed to close in seconds my logic's borders even more tightly
to anything new but dangerous,
anything original but subversive
that insisted on living in the world around me.

So for years I started my every day with great pleasure
stepping on the fragments of the person
I refused to become the day before just to satisfy my ego.
Thus I became those smiles of mine
I never found the courage to ask what I owe them,
the caresses I never let free to caress
any body I couldn't figure out what it wanted from my own.
So, despite being right next to it,
I never managed to touch, I never managed to really reach
the body of the person I loved
to be able to reassure it that the icy coating it sees,
whenever it manages to get past my coldness and touch me,
is not my truth but the defense my truth uses
so it won't appear to be less valuable than it could bear to be.

I left those parts of my soul
I never managed to acquire from my joy
out in the rain to rust, unused, forgotten
until I managed to convince them to break down
so they would never work again.
Right next to them I took out of my pockets
and left whichever important belief of mine
was pregnant with that hypocritical thought
that taught me how to be less human
without seeming to be less humane.

For the first time in my life
I became a refugee from my normality.
To avoid understanding
what my enthusiasm has been trying for years to confide in me
I spit in the face of my major advantages
and ran panic-stricken to get as far from me as I could.
I ran to hide in the last page
of the operating instructions my sorrow gave me as a gift
on that day of my adolescence during which my life
welcomed me to the first battle in which, by letting my ego win,

What does my defeatism want from me anyway?
Will I ever find out?

I would really like to know what those iron clouds
I have let freely sail in my sky want from me
hiding from me whenever they want any sunbeam I need to use
so that I may feel more optimistic than insignificant,
more pessimistic than perfect,
more exuberant blue than boring gray.
Souls really like to go near the edge of night
to the wastelands belonging to the minds of their owners
and without a worry in the world throw away the parts of their logic
that they themselves worshipped all day long.

Somewhere there in a cloud
made from the love of that gray that no longer believes in itself
and my shiest cry, the one that's made from the worst enemy
of a word that never wished to leave my mouth,
lives a tired shadow that's very important to me.
This aging shadow's only obligation
is to lie down every night between me and my fears
so it can figure out in which spot of the discontent I feel
about all that the day that just ended gave me as a gift
I hid the color I will use to paint my logic's wasteland
so that my mind can't clearly see and be disappointed by the dimensions
of everything it will be forced to dump during the night to fill it.
Hence this generous shadow manages every day
to unlock me from my sorrow
without forcing me to instantly rush to hide in
my freedom's brightest dungeon.

Pleased that I still can persuade my darkness
to use its finest techniques to hide me from my own ideals
and displeased that I can no longer convince my light
to show me how many of them I have already hurled
at the face of my future weakness,
I quickly rush to be in time to change the addresses in my mind
of the memories my future has already given me as gifts
before the events I will create them from even take place.
This way I want to stop my past from finding me
hoping that I will manage to conceal from my self-criticism
the huge mistakes I made yesterday
before dawn discovers them and brings them to me for breakfast.

with the next joyful hour of my life
about how much it is offering to buy me back from my shadow.
The well intentioned servant of my spinelessness
just acquired a cordial conversation partner
and my inadequacy its next hope.

My mistakes immediately realized what happened
and frantically ran using whatever means they had at their disposal
to get across to the opposite bank of the cheap reality
I was trying to manufacture at that time
out of any old useless piece of truth lying around me.
I barely had time to grab by its last letter
the toxic word that was trying to reach my mouth
so I could throw it down and prevent it from ruining me.

I want so much to get back.
I want so much to get back to the favorite places of my tranquility.
I want so much to get back to the favorite places of my tranquility
I can still understand what they mean to my happiness.
I need to because this way I will manage to talk
with those parts of my character
that can still stand being part of my personal free fall
without demanding to push me so I will fall into it.

to the asymmetry of the emotional ugliness
my mediocrity provides me with free of charge
without being able to understand
how every time I don't know how to feel
I almost voluntarily transform myself
into the most hard working porter
that my sorrow ever had at her disposal.

Wrestling for hours with the very tracks
my melancholy leaves behind,
an all-white teardrop jumped on me,
grabbed me from my soul's hands
and, donning all the troubles I had right then inside me,
gathered speed and dashed out of my eyes
to launch a kick that never stopped wearing an odd smile on its face
at the most tightly sealed windows my life has
and throw them wide open.
Oh, I want so much to learn how to hide
inside the secrets my happiness kept from me all these years!

I am ready to chop with the most aggressive axe I'll find
the screaming of the ugliness I constantly hear
gushing out of the raging darkness
that likes to live in the murkiest spot of my existence.
I want to become the secret messenger of the glory
which, for the sake of my next happiness,
my enthusiasm is willing to bring to life inside me.

I decided to lend to my decay
all that I owe to the remaining time of my life
and introduce myself again to the last daybreak
which insisted on taking a deep dive inside me
till it was able to help me understand
to the last everything my life wants to confide to me.

My heart is now sitting a self-taught hesitation away from me
and is demanding to shape my day from scratch
because the last real smile she saw at the edge of my mouth
was made of hundreds of prepaid pieces of joy
whose expiration date has long since passed.

In the absolute stillness
that only a very aggressive self-criticism
can secure from the world around me,
I can barely hear from afar the enormous engines
of the earth moving equipment that my sadness is using
to cut down any tree belonging to my happiness
repeatedly failing to start.
This must be the echo of the apology I owe to my future.

My laughter is ready to acquire the memory of my ambiguity.
The poor thing will be forced from now on
to borrow a footnote out of all those questions
the intelligence contained in every draw of my life
that never wanted to be included in my bio
wants to ask me.

I have to confess that I learned how to trust my mirror again
from watching the reflection of my body
on the part of the surface of my logic
that always insisted on being less smooth
so as to not make my life easier than it should be.
I will never forget what it had confided to me some years ago:
"First learn how to trust the lies of a mirror
before you decide to trust its opinion of you".
How right it was!
Perhaps the time has come for me to admit
that I fear the mirror's truth
but I dread, absolutely dread its lies.

Negotiating with any blurriness that can still stand to live on the surface
of the image my mirror is fashioning for me from scratch
I learned not to demand, but to endure.
From it I learned to never lock the door to the splendor
I often use to cover the ruins I'm made of
so they don't look so miserable.
I let that door be opened by the next breeze
that will blow from inside my soul,
the one that will come and ask
to lend it my wounds for a while so it can take care of them
and bring them back to me perhaps deeper
but certainly more honest.

Adding up all those early evenings I never lived
trying to teach my past how to remember the way I want
and my future how to forget the way my optimism wants to forget,
I let my self-confidence answer
all those questions it would never dare ask me.
Without realizing it, after a while I ended up
in the arms of a blue cube, or rather an almost cube
with the dimensions of a polite rejection by a generous insecurity
by a spotless conscience by a half erased "no".
These are the dimensions of the future
which the last proud silence that my scream hides inside it
wishes to give me as a gift.

You taught me to gently touch those emotions of mine
the previous midnight gave me
to look after till the end of the unexplainable happiness
which, having lived for a while in the most blurry reflection of my conscience,
doesn't know which road to take to come back to me.
Why should anyone try to discover what his various emotions contain
without knowing who he will become once he manages to touch them?

Whatever is whitest in me,
the kind of white that for years lived forgotten
at the borders of my optimism with the part of the sky
that it no longer wants to keep inside it,
decided all of a sudden to leap out of my body
and come find you to join with what's left of those rusty questions
your compassion has for months been doing all it can not to ask me.

Walking hand in hand with you at the limits
of the minimal white my life allows me to have
without being forced to betray the darkness
that had always stood by me through every trouble in my life,
you taught me not to feel unique
before I have a chance to first feel real,
not to become the emperor of my most complex melancholy
before I become the servant of my most linear kindness.

I sat for hours on my life's floor
and carefully removed from my feet
every last step I had ever put in them.
When I was finished, I immediately jumped up
and began to walk for hours in your footsteps,
the ones you had intentionally left at times behind
so I could someday feel, albeit briefly, the warmth, the humanity of each one of them
before my own reality could rush with all the strength in it
to freeze them, cover them, erase them.

Using a little of the light that tomorrow lets me have in me today
to see where I'm going,
I began to discover how many dreams
my personal spring can fit inside it
without the greyest day of November getting wind of it
and start taking them one by one
to deliver them tied hand and foot back to winter.

So you became the sunbeam that managed to fuse inside me
the beautiful silence with the illiterate cry,
the ugly word with the generous whisper,
the end of an ambiguity with the sweet answer of peacefulness,
a peacefulness that wants to give to its owner all the treasure it has in it
without keeping any for itself.

to exit my mouth without touching me.
My next decision has been patiently waiting for me for some time now
at the beginning of my most hypocritical glance
which in the next few seconds will try
with one fell swoop to grab from within the person I'm talking with
everything my mind was unable to for so long now.
Why does someone, considering them among the most precious he has,
continue to keep inside him those parts of his mind
that no longer want to help him think?
Do you think it's because there are moments in his life
when he knows it's best to fall in love with his silence more than any word,
prohibiting himself from making any decision?

I feel as if my gaze
has been observing me for hours from the opposite sidewalk
doing all it can to show me that it's more indifferent than indiscreet.
Maybe if I lived in an ideal world
I would know how to lose a fight
without it being obvious from the start that I felt more comfortable with a draw.
Or perhaps I'd know, without it being obvious that I did it on purpose,
how to lose those pages of the user's manual for myself
which cover how to think when I don't know how to feel
and how to feel when the time comes in one's life
when to survive emotionally he must stop thinking.
Do you think the moment has arrived when the first wrong decision of my day
will teach me how to behave impeccably during the rest of it?

I want to confide to you the agreement I made with myself.
We agreed that each time
I am unable to quickly figure out what I am feeling,
he will let me grow smaller until I manage to remain inconspicuous
even while passing through my own stupidity.
So now the time has come for me to realize
that every logic knows how to convince the soul
to love more that part of hers
that knows how to suffer better than any other.
Perhaps because it knows how to persuade a hope
that cannot squeeze between two shrewd hesitations
to go find another person's future to live in.

Ready to serve myself my next version
and the controversial reality after next
which I would do anything to be able to live in,
I cut up half of my most bankrupt lie
and shared its pieces with all the people
who happened to sit closer to my ambiguity than to me at the time.

I didn't know what to do, how to react!
I awkwardly took the five lonelinesses in hand
and immediately hung them on the hooks that were on the back side
of the only door to my soul in front of which someone would stand
only if he had no intension of ever opening it.
Behind this door lives that hope of mine
which I never taught how to hope more
without starting to betray my good qualities one by one.
There also lives the last sterilized whisper my courage contains
which fears me more than it fears the part of my weakness
I hid inside it during that night when,
to prevent my truth from defeating me,
I rushed to hide behind my gravest error.

A man destined to lose
starts at the beginning of every fight
to denounce his good qualities one by one to his cowardice.
In contrast, a winner always finds a new way
to temporarily conceal his shortcomings
behind the brightest side of his courage.
Ah, what must one do
to be able to permanently erase from his memory
those nights when, to avoid being defeated by the meaning of his life
while competing with himself,
he always ran to hide behind his most ambitious mistake
and ultimately ended up coming in second!
What anger. What terrible inadequacy!

Searching for the reason I am not happier
I realized that I shouldn't always wait with open arms
to welcome all the misery my life sends right at me.
Today I have no need of any more unhappiness.
I let all the "maybes" that have been circling around me since this morning
paint the hours and the minutes
on the first avenging questions my beliefs want to ask me
and start walking backwards to the last dawn in my life
that didn't know at what point of the day it should transform itself
to help me get through it safe and sound.

It's so excruciating to feel like you wake up in the morning
facing a dawn which, if it had a choice of which part of the day it would want to be,
would rather be midnight!
Perhaps it's time I stopped giving my life as gifts
downhills that are smarter than me.

even when the smallest of candles is lit near it.

All night I couldn't stop making copies of a totally blank page
which, refusing to go to sleep before me,
kept staring at me with questioning eyes.
A little later I fell asleep next to a dream
that loved its silence more than mine.

Leaving my mind free to follow
the frenzied rhythm of absolute silence
which only those ambiguous conversations with one's self can offer,
I overtook whichever part of my truth
seeks to daily worship any other chaos but mine,
borrowed myself from my most carnivorous weaknesses,
introduced myself to the mud that clung to my footsteps
during my strolls in the part of my past
that has decided to begin tomorrow,
sat next to the frightened purple twilight
so it could teach me how to love the mistakes
the white side of my black and white ego
intends to make on my behalf real soon,
and started looking for the dream police
so they can nab me getting smashed
drinking the residue of the dreams
I've refused to dream all these years.

Hearing the pleas of the night,
which for days now has been insistently painting
with colors of its own choosing
my optimism on the surface of my own eyes,
I tried to convince my ego to let me speak
with the part of myself that was left over
from that endless fight with my self-control.
I thus fell asleep inside the back pocket of the least real hope
my soul could produce at that hour.

Night's end is now ready to hand me over to my own beginning.
The end of my self-confidence is now ready to hand me over
to the interpretation of my life.
A new chapter in an age-old story
is ready to fall in love with the side of myself
I never felt was truly mine.

In the incoherence of the moment,
I search, as fast as I can, for any emotion of mine
that today will finally manage on my behalf to take by storm the glass fortress
where my reality runs to hide every morning to avoid meeting me.

I continue feverishly negotiating with yesterday's truth
trying to sell it the percentage of my luck
that still wants to belong to me.
Synchronized with the sun's first light
I start repairing, as fast as I can, my shadow's damages
which I inflicted on it yesterday
so it can withstand living at my side for another day.

Meanwhile, the new day rushes to hide those secrets of mine
that only have a few hours to learn how to properly lie.
Enough. I am just tired of giving private lessons to my cowardice
every opportunistic morning of my life
on how to handle those virtues of mine it can't figure out
whether it fears them more
than it wants to love them.

I'm tired of displaying like a street peddler every morning
my old victories on a cart
hoping that during the day I'll manage to convince
the people around me to take them in their hands to inspect them
and then make me an offer to buy them from my sorrow,
and with them, me as well.

Today I'll teach my day to dream the dreams
the bankrupt nighttime lends it each daybreak,
the ones I throw into the trashcan
of the first good-morning I'll utter.
It's already 8:15, the sun just managed to overcome its initial hesitations
and I'm still not the absolute owner of the shadow
I will dutifully drag behind me all day.

Let me become the Trojan horse-like words
which for so many years my own phrases hid inside them
and charge through the front gate of my melancholy,
not to conquer it, but just to allow myself to touch it.

I am now ready to surrender to the rest of my life
all that I was not able up to now to love.
I sense time's unruly tentacles
weaving around the illicit shadow that my terrified logic spread around her
to hide what she's been afraid to embrace for so long.
So I learned from an early age how to entertain myself
before each time I ended up surrendering
to the boredom of my own normality.

I am now finally ready to become one,
maybe even to be absorbed by everything
which since I was twenty I avoided hating.
It seems that a minute of spring
finally managed to find some incredible courage in it
and, holding a single serene sunray in hand,
set out to defeat the entire winter.

I don't want any more to blindly follow
the path of compromise that my inadequacy has carefully carved for me.
I want to strike with all the heart I have in me at my own sorrow,
convince all the smiles I keep in me to flow out my lips
and spread to the world around me
all the happiness they themselves feel.

Every time the rules of my life,
those ruthless dictators of my happiness,
bring me a blank piece of paper and demand that I write down
all that I was never able to understand,
after staring at it for few minutes,
I always turn it on the other side
and start writing all that I was ever able to feel.

I won't let those rules write my life's operating instructions
so that every time I do something that is not in them
they can cast those besieging looks of theirs at me,
hoping they'll be able this way to immobilize me
in their moral desolation.

I want to do my best to persuade my time
to change the way it calculates what I owe it,
because before becoming an arsonist
I want to learn how to be a really good firefighter.

suddenly stopped, turned around and said to me:
"Reaching a point in your life
where you are tired of thinking is simply a defeat.
Reaching a point where you are tired of feeling is a disaster."
Before I had time to reply, it quickly asked me:
"Why did you build a heart out of everything you didn't understand in your life?"

When I no longer knew what other way to use
to be able to start feeling again,
I immediately began to wrap my body with my most unsatisfied questions,
then grabbed from inside me what I thought at the time
was the most timid end of the sky
and wrapped it like a sheet as tightly as I could around my heart.
I did not want to hurt her, just to make her realize
how useful a despair can be which wants so much to succeed
that it starts constantly transforming itself
until it manages to become the next ambition.

I picked up speed and with it rolled around for hours
on my first thought I couldn't quite complete
until I stumbled on the point in my life
where all the fearless answers given to me by the gold dust
I frequently use to beautify anything I cannot make right
go every afternoon to meet
the questions it is afraid to ask me.

When we separated I took all the courage
my heart had no other use for right then,
walked to the most fearful edge of the meaning of my life
and started placing my hopes one next to another
to make a joy out of everything in me that is no longer sad,
to make a sky out of everything in me that is no longer blue.
I want so much to persuade the sky to let me store in its deepest parts
some of my most precious dreams,
those I always thought that I could never live away from.
These are those dreams of mine that want to fly up high
so they can feel even for just a few moments
that they will never need to land again.
Will I be, I wonder, able to drag out of my mouth
the bankrupt answer I ought to give to the persistent questions
of what appears to be the new central truth of my life?
I doubt it.

that in only a few seconds can transform
a simple song into a soul's anthem.
I am talking about that song whose enchanting tune
my soul has been trying to learn for quite some time
so she can sing it to me the next time
she'll see me being grabbed by my most destructive insecurities
so they can remake me from scratch
into something that looks more like a disguised winner
than a real loser.

The sky though is still resisting.
The part of the moon that doesn't belong to it yet
is struggling with all the strength it has saved inside it
to defeat the last exhausted rays of the sun
which have already started to flicker because they want to go to sleep.
It digs like mad to rip out of my soul the soil that the end of the night gave birth to
to try to cover up all that happened to me overnight
with which it didn't agree.

Along with that, it wants to wash out from inside me
all those memories I intentionally left unexplored
so that I won't be forced to make them mine.
They are the ones that demand to beget for a second time
the ten biggest phobias I would never want to have.

My breaths and my words are fighting about which one will be the first
to show me in what direction I should turn my soul
so that I will able to distinguish my new self
among all the older ones.
With every second that goes by
time spawns new questions which not even itself will try to understand
before infinity comes dragging behind it enormous velvet bags
filled with answers that refuse to introduce themselves to me
before they figure out who I am not.

I gathered around me all the stray emotions I've thrown out of my body
and took the gag off my heart's mouth.
How much can a person grow in two minutes?
How much can he learn about his sadness in three?

Half sunk in the dreams I hope not to lose
before I have time to dream them until the end,
I realize that my beauty is made by my truth,
not my sorrow that has constantly been carrying
a shadow's distance behind me
what my courage calls the "rest of myself".
Naked before the integrity of my silence
I fear no one, not even those emotions of mine I haven't felt yet.
Freed from all that wishes to free me
I drank two gulps of a very peaceful early evening
and started to methodically gather the pieces of my hopes
I have mistakenly been throwing away
in the gutters of my optimism.

which today, for the first time in my life,
I feel like I no longer want to represent.

from the pockets of the souls of the people around him
will make him happy.
What wouldn't a soul do to leave its pockets deliberately undarned!

I'm so hurt by the future happy moments of my life
that have long declared that they'll do all they can to never be mine.
While I waited for my most battle-ready mistakes to gather around
hoping I might persuade them to help me answer
everything you avoided asking me last night,
I began to talk to my ego, with my vanity unable to overhear.
The crafty devil, realizing the state I was in,
had already been sitting down for some time now awkwardly far from me
as if afraid to talk to me,
because that might have forced it to admit that it belonged to me.
Do you think that this could be a good opportunity to get to know my ego better,
in case I might finally realize how much more than what it asks of me
is all that I've been asking it to give me all these years?

My heart today wants to have only two colors.
Probably because a part of hers seems happy,
the rest of her does all it can to be sad.
Is this actually possible?
I'm almost sure that in a certain spot of hers
I've hidden an enormous joy and in another a huge misery,
I simply can't remember where,
and the worst thing is that I worry that if she finally lets me find one of them,
she might run as fast as she can to hide the other one from me forever.

Why does man start looking at his other emotions
only after he gets tired of looking his sorrow in the eyes?
Unfortunately I do the same thing.
For hours now I've been admiring the moon
for how well it handles its faint light.
How I wish sometime towards the end of its shift
it would let me sit even for just a few minutes right beside it
so we're both next to each other,
and show me how to handle the little light I can still keep in me.
Oh, how I wish I could handle my loneliness as well as it does!

How can I start answering the endless questions
the darned thing has been asking me for days
while it keeps hiding behind every new minute of my life
that refuses to give me all the time it contains
before I manage to explain to it what exactly I am going to ask it to do on my behalf?

Will I ever figure out what the hell my time wants from me?
I might discover the answer the first time I find within me
the courage to refuse to look into the mirror
time sets up in front of my face
each time it sees me not knowing how to rebuff
the most ardent kisses of my defeatism.
Then again I might find the answer whenever I realize
that every wrinkle of my body is another question time wishes to ask my vanity,
a question my happiness gave it to ask me
because I refused to answer her.
Maybe that's why my heart has more wrinkles
than any other part of my body.

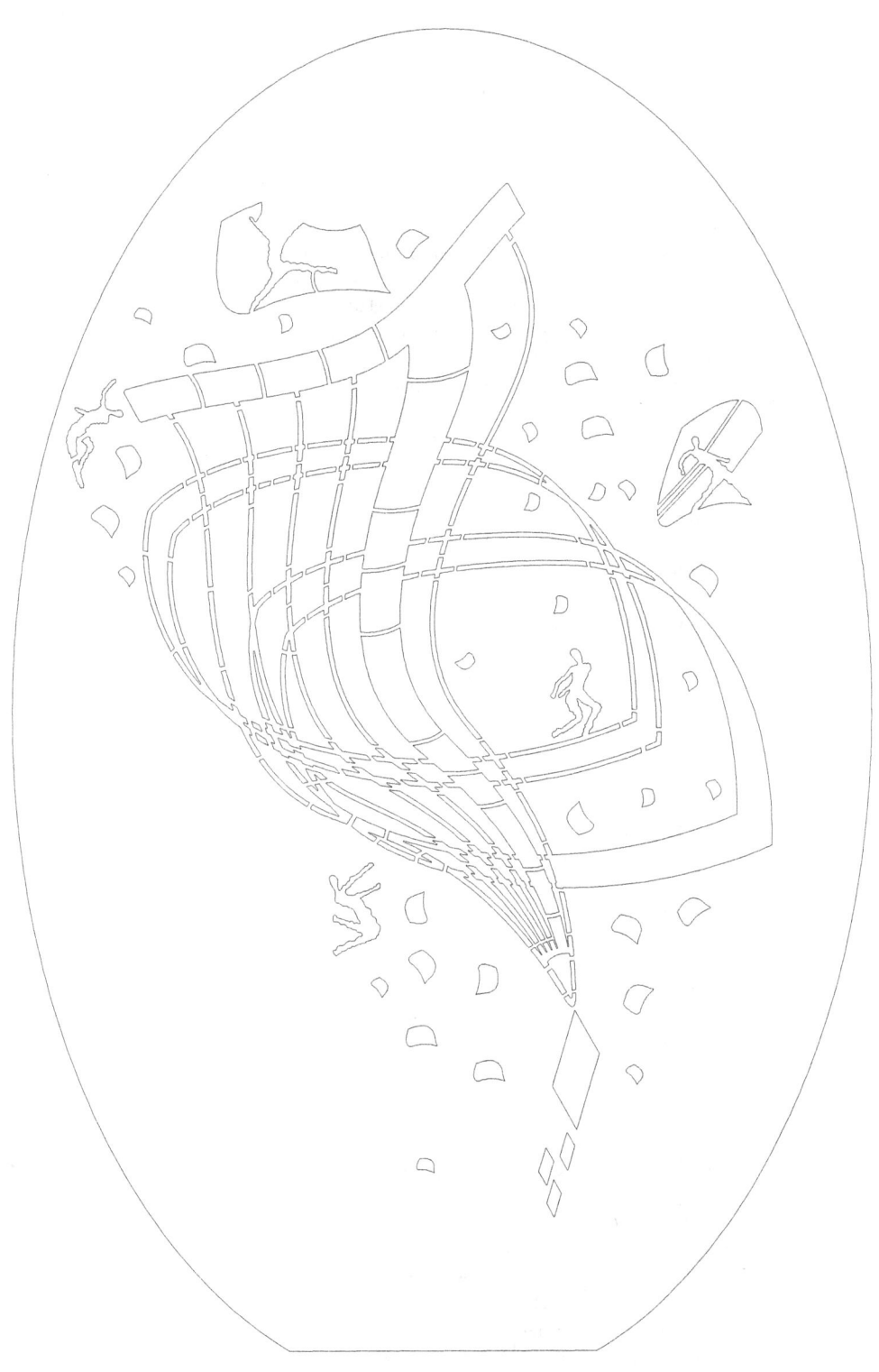

Could this be the naïve but invaluable definition of love?
In the emotionally condensed stillness of a relationship that doesn't know how to hide
any shared feeling we both can't understand why we feel it anymore,
we let our words run parallel to each one's intelligence
so they won't cast shadows behind them,
they won't leave evidence that at one time they actually crossed our minds.

Relationships are very good at finding ways to end before their expiration date.
While looking through the ruins of our reality to find the reason this happens,
an emotion we both felt at the same time
totally dilapidated due to excessive use,
detached from a spot in our souls
which our eyes didn't have time to see and crashed into us.
It stepped with all the strength it had in it
on our first common footstep it found in its way,
which had long since rusted due to disuse,
and chewing an old smile of mine like a bubble gum
came and rolled towards your heart,
then took a spectacular spin around your body,
and sat right in front of it.

"Both of you follow me,
and I will show you what you always thought you couldn't bear to look at"
it said in a hoarse, tired voice,
a voice that had probably just awakened after many years
from within the part of our courage most willing to help us.
Our eyes followed this exhausted emotion,
with us unable to physically do so,
taking a peculiar route through any thoughts of ours
that at the time were trying to find a way to let us produce them
without ending up being frightened
by what we'd become if we tried to make them our next reality.

Our eyes walked for hours till they arrived
in front of an amazingly shiny purple coffin.
At first they were reluctant to look at it,
but the emotion insisted.
Embarrassed, they took a few uneasy steps forward
unable to help us understand how it is possible
since the ground they stood on was completely flat,
that they should feel like they're standing in the middle of a vast downhill
that wouldn't let anyone else traverse it
apart from the greatest sorrow of those who never dared descend it.

in the midst of which two spotless white rowboats
were competing hard against each other
trying to cross it as fast as they could.

Each one had twelve hardened rowers
and a single passenger in the bow
who sat slightly higher than the rest of the crew.
In this position in one boat sat the sun
and in the other a moon that was two days old.
The race's judge was standing on a skinny light pink question mark
that was sitting right in the middle of the coffin
and was waiting to be entertained
by anyone trying to find out in which part of the sky
it had hidden the grand answer.

Next to this question mark stood a euphoric hope
while an extremely beautiful but slightly sad misgiving
sat in an extremely uncomfortable, very small chair.
For those few moments these two
were for us the most precious things in the world.
When does a coffin become more comfortable than a bed?
When does a relationship become more uncomfortable than its own end?
Perhaps when its beginning finds the courage to confide to us
what it kept hidden inside it through the years.
You see, in a relationship, if you manage
to carefully unwrap without breaking
from inside the common memories you have
the very first look one gave to the other
you will find in it its expiration date.

Am I worth the mistakes I will never make?
I will probably find out after spending long hours
correcting anything right I didn't manage to accomplish in my life.
Maybe it's time to admit that I never stopped using the kind of truth
that helps me keep my self-esteem satisfied.

I'm haunted by everything in my life I left unfinished
because I didn't know how to demolish it completely.
When a heart's stains demand to be even cleaner than her.
You know, for a long time I lived the kind of life
that no longer respects the mistakes it's made of.

The most uncomfortable beds are made of wood and jealousy!
Don't worry, whichever part of your life you don't understand
your body soon will.
I'm not sure but I think that our common abyss
would like to fit one more misery.

When defeats no longer know how to speak,
victories start not remembering how to keep quiet.
The moment in a relationship
when its favorite word stops being "hello"
and is replaced by "goodbye".
When two people let the biggest "zeroes" that live inside them
grab the steering wheel of their life and drive it to the next dead end.

How will I manage to peel away my last hope
from the back side of my character flaws?
A truth just came and announced to me
that it can't bear to fit half-finished words inside it anymore.
For years I have been practicing daily
how not to be my best self.

Mixing up the different realities
your luck dropped in my palm
I accidentally caught the only one that didn't want to be mine.
Who told you that my hopes no longer need you today?
I really love listening to you making my past
promises that you never intend to keep.

decide to reenter our eyes
to arrive at the beginning of our next fight ahead of us.

On the way to becoming better
I broke my personal paradise in two
to find out what my adolescence had hidden in it.
What I feel whenever I have nothing better to do
than be my sorrow's next conversational partner.
I went and sat at that point in our relationship
where those of its truths that want to live only in our future
don't grow anymore.

You just told me one of those phrases
that have the disgusting power
to instantly put a full stop to an entire summer.
To see how tough I've become,
I asked my tenderness to let me rest for a while at the place of its birth.
Trying to figure out who I become
each time I can't stand being the employee of my most ruthless thought.

Holding the dictionary of my nakedness I began to undress.
The time of night when my heart learns how to hide
among the secrets of my previous serenity.
Our relationship has no more tokens of joy to insert in its future
so it will dispense to us from inside it small portions of prepackaged happiness.

Lips that behave as if they never understood the raison d'être
of any smile they created themselves.
In closing, please let me affix my sorrow
between the two times in our fight
when we didn't know how to hurt each other any more
without starting to betray our own beliefs.
Do you think this is the way
a breath which never believed in the honesty of the words
it is forced to convey
embraces hearts?

Here, take back all the notes
my melancholy kept all these years
during every one of our fights.

describing an event that started and finished in the past,
one that was over before someone starts remembering it.
To my surprise I discovered that day
that there are some memories that refuse to come to an end
the moment the event that created them is over,
forcing it to live forever stuck between the part of the mind
that generates the most optimistic thoughts
and the one that gives birth to the most defective hopes.

The memories that know how to hurt more than others
always carry in the vaguest spot inside them
an extremely timid but toxic "almost".
It's this almost which,
gushing up whenever it wants from the depths of the past,
comes to both besiege the present with its questions
and apologize to the future
for all the misery it will soon start causing it.

I really fear those cathartic "almosts" in my life
which I myself had nailed with great effort
one by one on the back of the door to my past
that suddenly and unexpectedly break free from it
and lunge at breakneck speed right at me
to pull me by the collar,
stand me up before the whitest wall of my life
and start reminding me who I really am.
What a struggle, what an endless struggle for man
against all those "almosts" he packed his bio with
so that the reader cannot figure out
behind which of his words his truth tries to hide
and before which of his acts his lies will burst out.

When will I finally realize that the various "almosts" I utter,
pouring gas so they can set on fire
the man I would like to be tomorrow,
end up doing good only to my self-indulgence?
Each one returns hours after I uttered it to besiege me
believing that my truth belongs first to it and then to me
and demand of me to give it back.
At the same time it comes to apologize
because it's looking for a way to acknowledge how much it has hurt me
each time when, by using its huge invisible curtain
it was able to hide reality from my enthusiasm
thus forbidding my good qualities to take the next step
and grab from my future whatever is theirs.

It has caused me so much pain, so much agony!
Perhaps even more than all the different "nos" I said in my life
that managed with their inimitable technique
first to slam doors in my face one after another
before they successfully threw open the most interesting consciences.

the cowardice they nurture inside them
and persuade it to emerge from behind the back of truth
where it's been hiding for some time now?
Is today the day that lies will stop trying
to find out in which part of reality they lost their favorite words?
Today is most probably the day
when humble questions will start trying to figure out
at which point of the discussion with myself
they should try to hide their vain answers.

I will find out soon.
Maybe the time has come when truths will realize
that they detest delusions more than they detest lies.
For a long time now I've been trying to explain to my words
that by listening, without talking,
you have time to understand, you have time to assess
what the silences of the person you're talking to are trying to hide from you
and most importantly, what your own silence is trying to hide from you.

As soon as I stopped listening and started talking
I felt like I immediately began
to fall in love with the phony wisecracks I made up myself,
a short time later with the meaningless phrases I uttered
and finally the genuine nonsense I left unsaid.
So I always ended up giving birth to the great delusion
which sooner or later challenged before your very eyes
my honesty to a duel on which of the two
would first manage to deprive my logic of her right
to start describing to you in detail everything I avoided saying to you
so that a bit later I could let the part of my melancholy
that no longer fits to live in my soul
explain it to you much better than I could.

While we were talking I saw what's left of my mind
once you remove its falsest arguments
stretch its long, skinny hand towards you
to slap your soul before it starts telling her
what's on the pages of its operating manual
that were left deliberately blank.

Anything I hesitate or fear to feel
tumbles amid those words
which my enthusiasm begs me to say
and my self-preservation to hide.
I feel like I no longer fit in every word I utter.
I don't even fit in the part of that phrase
my cry has crammed between my mind and my mouth
so it has time to finish giving it the sound it wants.

Looking into each other's eyes
we let all those huge, heavily armed "I cannot" we brought with us
to protect our self-preservation from our compassion
run faster than us.
We really want them to trip us up
so that we won't manage to transform
into what our kindness would really want us to be.
Meanwhile, any of my emotions that cannot find a way to persuade my mouth
to carry it to the ears of the people I love
decides to stay forever inside me
to prove to me in front of everyone how cold I really am.

If we weren't already deserters from our own image
would we be able to become castaways of our essence?
Would we be able to shipwreck in that spot of the sky that is least dangerous of all,
the one that till today has never produced a single thunderbolt from its bowels?
Why does man have to be the prisoner of the one question he fears to ask himself?
It's not by accident that every time I could no longer figure out a way
to handle the questions of my happiness
I stretched my hand upwards as far as I could
and grabbed the most optimistic blue the sky had at the time in it
to force it to enwrap my biggest insecurity with its body
hoping it might manage to temporarily hide it from me.

I am left alone with those thoughts of mine I can no longer think.
I watch my emotionally greediest thoughts
survive by easily passing through the tempest
caused by those verbal fights that know how to extract
an incredibly thorny finish out of a velvety start
and I despair.
I really fear those duels at the end of which
you try for hours to find out whether your skillful verbal strikes
ended up hurting you more than your opponent!
Who said that malice, having satisfied itself by wrecking anything it finds before it,
won't eventually turn against its own owner?

to be able to so easily defeat my own wounds
while playing their favorite game?
The most primal impasses of my arrogance
are ready in the last breath of air that the twilight breaths
to reveal their attractive figures
and excite any carnal agony
my stupidity continues to have.

Tomorrow's wretchedness refuses to enter the same ring
to fight with my dignity
which, as soon as she saw me coming straight at her,
pulled down her zipper and took out from inside her
the latest shinning version of who I believe I could become
if I got rid of my most optimistic shortcomings.

Meanwhile the chains with which I tie my dignity every morning
so she won't try to get away from me,
continue to gloat about their supremacy in the corner of the ring
which has started to act less like a corner
and more like a hideout.
I wonder, would I dare live a life
without the daily help of my greatest flaws?
If so, why don't I?

Trying to become the locksmith of the ghosts that live inside me
I fastened myself to the meaning of those light purple words
that love my secrets more than I do,
those words that keep on aimlessly wandering
somewhere between my mind and my mouth
waiting for me to think them up so that they may help me lose the fight
and gain my serenity.

These are the last words I utter
each time I surrender to my arrogance total control over my mouth,
these words that are always eager,
solely for the enjoyment of my previous ego,
to go up and down the elevator of my ambition as many times as required.

They are prepared to keep on doing it
till the people that happen to be next to me at the time
are able to feel that in the moment's ingratitude
a past will be born that is more proud of me
than the one I have now.
So yet another day is preparing itself to end
during which I managed to pass unnoticed
among my most important advantages.

What makes me think that I alone discovered the secret door
time uses to make me believe
that I can go back to my past
without insulting the moment I am experiencing right then by spitting in its face?
How on earth haven't I realized that for some time now
the next moment of my life has stopped caring about me?

I don't care because I have the impression that it doesn't believe me anymore.
I don't realize that it's the one that first managed
to discover the secret door which for some time now
my ego has been building in the least visible walls inside me
so it can get to my insecurities faster than I can.
Do you think this might be the self-rescinding apology of my age?
Or is it the tyranny of a delusion
that was born smarter than its owner?

Seeing that she won't manage today once again
to pass through the most doubtful drop of sweat
that's rushing right now to get out of my body,
my heart convinced me to make a u-turn on the highway of time
and fall on my knees to beg forgiveness
from the apology I owe my courage
for all the things I haven't even tried to do in my life.

The worst sound someone can hear
is this total silence I am hearing right now
while traversing the next minute of my life
without knowing that, by squeezing even the sad moments of the day,
I might manage to get a little joy out of them.
This damned sound tears my ears into a thousand pieces
just by reminding me how incapable I am
to discover the joy I already have in my soul.
At the same time I let the anxiety I feel about the future
surge uncontrollably inside me cutting my conscience in half
to find out which other part of my past it can fit in her.

Doing all I can to avoid becoming an accomplice of my biggest weakness
I finally reach that part of my fears
which they themselves admit is their darkest one,
the part which, unable to do anything to prevent it,
I have personally taken care of as well as I could for years.
They come one by one and lie right next to my body
so that each one can mate with a different part of my pessimism.
Panicked, my logic vainly rushes back and forth
trying to find a way to throw them out,
hoping to give me another chance
to shield my serenity from the blurry dreams
my malice left for me a few hours ago on my nightstand.

only in the part of my soul that wants to be happy
before it tries to find out what other emotions it already has in it!

By the corpses of the two emotions I just killed
so that I won't force myself to feel closer
to that part of my detachment which in the past
has generated more profit for me than any other of my traits,
I realized yet again how much more ambitious than my joy
my sorrow can be.

Not having any other spot in my mind to go to,
I hid behind the promises I made to it that I will live a life during which
I will serve my guilt before I start serving my thoughts.
When I felt that I wasn't in danger any more,
I began to aimlessly wander among the questions my questions have
hoping I might finally convince them
to start treating with more respect
the recycled answers given to them by the trophies my insecurities won.

Having reached the point in my life
where the start refuses to become an end
I started spitting on the sidewalk to make my own mud
just in case I managed to see the most truthful image
someone can create by using his own illusions:
himself down on his knees in the middle of a puddle of muddy water
begging any part of his he does not understand
to show him where he should go.

Each of us is a revolution of good.
Each of us is a revolution of good
that must first defeat the evil that's inside him
before he starts fighting the evil around him.

Each one of us must start his own revolution
regardless if the person beside us agrees, is indifferent or is set against it.
If we succeed, then we will end up living in a world
where kindness will replace meanness,
honesty will replace lies, a caress will supplant the fist,
compassion will displace distrust, beautiful words will replace curses.
We shouldn't let others begin the revolution
and then simply follow
letting it pass before us and grab us by the hand
to pull us where we should have already gone.

Start now!
Break in half the sturdiest "if" you host inside your mind,
the one you could never stand up to,
and discover the part of your mind
you have already hidden inside it.
Don't forget that a man who has victory inside him
walks in front of his courage,
while one who is destined to lose
has already started walking behind his cowardice.

Holding a dream in our right hand
let's heave and tear down the next step they gave us to set on our legs
so we can create it ourselves from scratch
because the most beautiful dreams
are built from the ashes of an ugly reality.
Let's finally stop lowering our head
whenever our apathy gives us those stern looks
forcing us to take that damn spineless step sideways
every time we see malice, injustice or ugliness
rushing straight at us.

Come, let's replace the last silence with the first word,
the pre-worn delusion with the vitality of a brand new truth,
the most seductive fist we have been nurturing in our body for years now
with our most kindhearted compassion.
Questions of my truth, if you wish to do something for me
stop following me, go past me and show me the way
so I can traverse the main avenue inside my head
without raising the kind of dust that will not demand to soil everything around me
to make it seem less beautiful, less authentic.

that winter always left unguarded,
shove away all your old defeats that keep on admiring you,
toss in the sewers of your life
all the black you discovered while exploring its white,
wash off your body the finger marks left on it
by all the midnights that tried to abduct you
from who you were at the end of each day of your life
to drag you back to that part of your sorrow
where you can bear to live without understanding exactly what you feel,
and allow any belief of yours you haven't looked in the eyes for years
to return from the next blank page
which your life proudly displays in front of your face
and thrust its hand into the most unexplored pocket of your soul
to pull out from inside it the taste of your future self
that makes you prouder than any other.

Life of mine, please tell me,
tell me that the time has come for me to feel deep inside me
that happiness is an uncharted walk on a stretched wire rope
held up on one side by the safety of mediocrity
and on the other by the insecurity of beauty.

This is not my last breath.
This is not my last page.
This is not my last compassion.
This is not my last happiness.

and stays completely alone with his silence,
after a while he starts hearing that unbreakable song that comes out of the dreams
those wounds of his that can stand to be more ambitious than him
have the right to dream.

How crafty my wounds are!
They don't stop telling me about how they would like to heal
if I ever allowed them to dream for themselves and not on my behalf.
So, listening to all the invaluable advice dawn had to give me,
I began to contrive the triumphant ending my pain would like to have.
Because fogs are made of thoughts that never dared to end,
the more I kept thinking,
the more I surrendered to the hands of the fog
which since the day before yesterday I had wanted so much to create myself
so I can donate it to the future my vanity would like to have
if it ever managed to convince me to live a life
which from its first minute wouldn't owe anything to my sorrow.

Filled with an odd sense of nervousness,
I picked up from the floor as quickly as I could
some dusty words I had dropped long ago
and tossed them as far back as I could in my mouth.
They were all the words I had decommissioned myself
because they never found the courage in them to make me speak,
not to defend what I am,
but to defend what I never became.
Right after that I started reading to my optimism
the technical characteristics of the latest fear
I just discovered I acquired.

Before noon, my hollow triumphs, without trying to,
had already become the afternoon's favorite children.
Without me understanding why,
since it wouldn't start work for several more hours,
the brand new night opened the door
and burst into my day, into my life
and the first thing it did was to hang the first darkness
yesterday's midnight had given me as a gift
on the sole hanger in my soul it found free.

Trying to answer the only question
my soul hasn't asked me yet,
I hung from my most untalkative truth
on which the sky had stumbled a few minutes ago
trying to find out at which spot of the joy I feel it ends.
When he forgets how to move ahead
why does man fall at the feet of his ego so it can teach him how to hope again?
Perhaps because a vanity's bill
includes the dreams of the ambiguity she ordered herself from her owner's future.

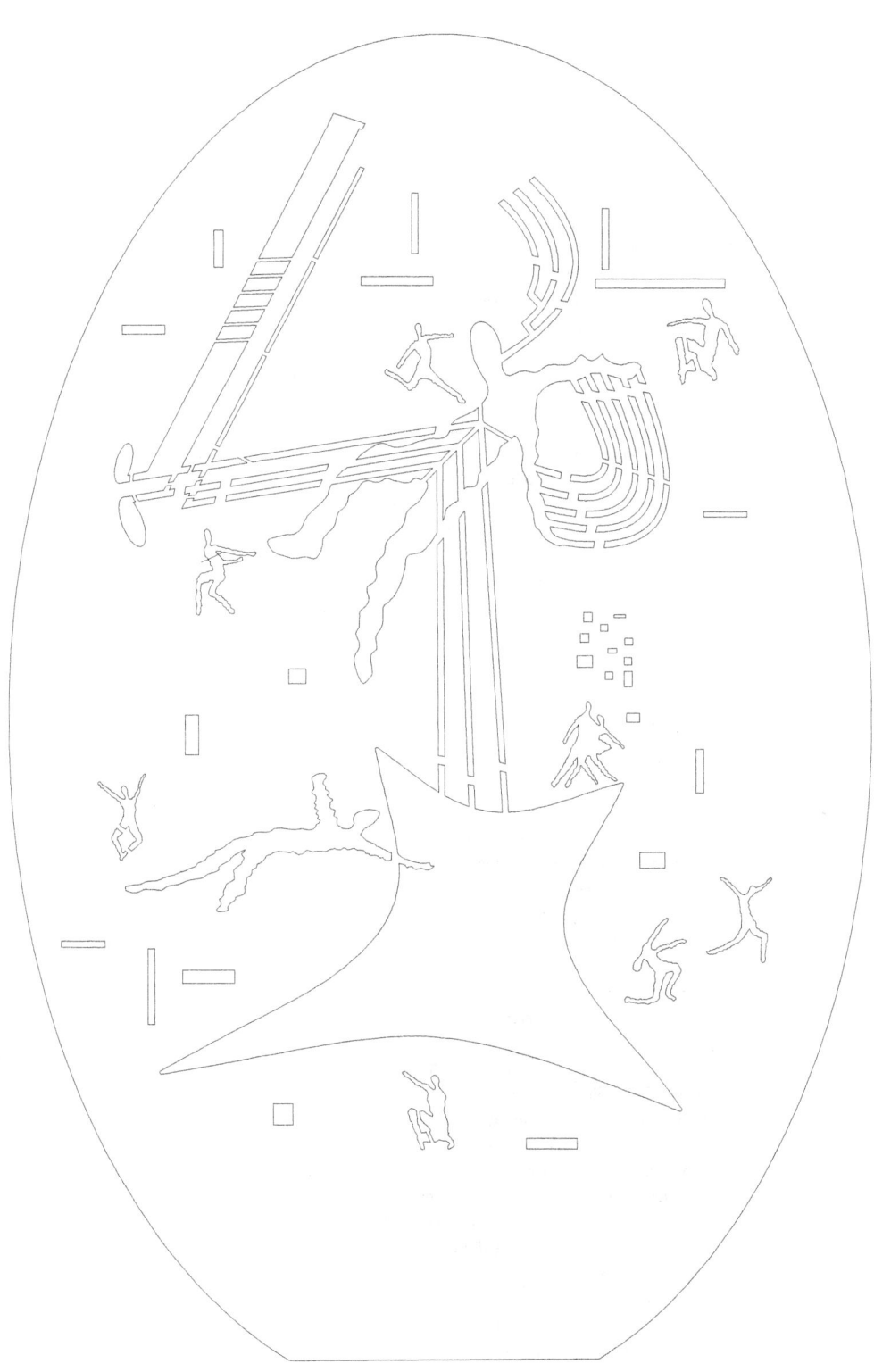

until the sky is left all alone in the middle of the universe totally naked?
Perhaps I'll be able to find out when for the first time in my life
I'll feel comfortable lying down next to my own nakedness
without demanding something from her.
Seeking a dusk that's willing to hang out with my melancholy
I started walking alongside, but at an increasingly slower pace,
the questions my hopes wanted to ask me at the time.

I couldn't keep up with their tempo
and soon after ended up losing them
somewhere amidst anything I felt right then
that preferred to be truly pathetic
rather than falsely optimistic.
Meanwhile, staring me for hours in the eyes
every next step of mine I was considering not taking
made me understand that each time in the past few days
I ended up secretly talking to my cowardice
I helped it realize how much it despises me.

I feel as if my every step,
even when it treads on the most solid ground it can find,
devises a brand new kind of mud to get stuck in,
to be thoroughly immobilized.
It does all it can to not reach that spot
where my hopes have confided to it
that it will be able to find those dreams of mine
my adolescence dreamt on my behalf
at a time of my life when it still believed that it would last forever.
How I wish I had the wisdom when I was sixteen
to fall at the feet of my logic
and beg it to allow my adolescence to never end!

Happy is the man whose dreams talk directly to his footsteps
without him being able to interfere!
Being more confused than pessimistic
but also more optimistic than free,
I tried to pick up the first truth I found sitting across from me
scrutinizing me with that strange look
which only one's great truths have the right to look him over with.
While she tried to figure out if she's belongs more to me
than I belong to her,
I jumped up in time to grab her and instantly nailed her
to the most conscientious edge of that decision of mine
I want so much to persuade to become the center of my next victory.

They are the ones I tossed into the trashcans
my future made sure to leave for me at every spot of my life I passed by
each time I found the courage to spit in the face
of the dreams my past had about me without my permission.

Trying to unlock my eyes
from staring first at the false uniqueness of my past
and then at the woman I want to love,
I persuade my optimism to ask her a question
whose answer I buried long ago
somewhere between the end of my ego and the beginning of its disappointment
for those successes I never managed to offer it.

By God, I never managed to realize
the grave danger my soul faced
from the attacks of my self-confidence
except for those moments when, in the aftermath of victory,
amid the cries coming out of the distorted by its guilt applause
and the barren silence that came out of my ulterior motives,
I momentarily believed that I was more half wrecked than half built.
Ah, how can one be happy
living amid what the red carpet of his ego is asking him to do for it
and the trash the very same red carpet
likes to frequently give birth to in the center of his own dignity?

Realizing its own angle the uphill was disappointed.
My cry itself learned long ago
how to tear, if need be, its body in two
to find out about today's free offers
which my advantages advertise to those people around me
who still don't realize how much worse than what I show I really am.

And I, in order to try and discover which part of my dignity
the emotionally most distant part of my embrace is selling today,
will start leaving one by one my life's colors
in each of my own steps that I abandon behind me
because I just can't figure out what it is that it wants from me.
It's these steps which my victories
will leave with me all night to look after,
the ones that know so well how to build
three walls and a conscience
to lock me up forever inside them.

Seeing the myriad different imprints of my right foot
I left behind in the mud
that my cowardice made especially for my future to step on,
I realize that all these years I've been surrounded
by these black and blue theories
which never permitted me to figure out
that my hopes are colorblind.
I've made up my mind.
Tonight I will marry off my shyest miracle
to the part of the moon that always believed in me.

While I listen to the malfunctions of my vagueness
recite one by one the silken monologues
which the gray end of my logic taught them,
I start untangling from inside me
the fist of a soul which is ready to test her strength
by grabbing my fears one by one by the waist
and kissing them as passionately as she can on the mouth.

because they always managed to convince me not to shout them.

I no longer feel daily the obligation to honor my sorrow.
I donned my smile like a last piece of clothing over my own fears
and laughing my heart out,
I entered those half-demolished rooms of my soul
that remember how to give birth to the kind of happiness
which I still don't know how to feel.

I am trying so hard to sell to you?
The gift I gave you has been afraid to smile at you for hours now
because it doesn't know what to feel,
perhaps also because it doesn't know what it will make you feel,
even though it was told at the store of handmade consciences
where I bought it to treat you kindly.

I was surprised that you didn't hesitate to open it for a single moment
even though while tearing the wrapping you saw written on the ribbon:
"EMOTIONS EXCHANGE STORE.
We assure you that our merchandise will manage to buy from
the people you're interested in any emotion you want,
otherwise we'll give you a full refund."
A man's intelligence has so many deep, dark, vulnerable spots
to hide all that it will never be able to understand!

Hearing the arguments of my malice
screaming as loud as they can in my ears,
I try to leave you alone, helpless, hoping you'll be able to figure out
what the gift I sent to conquer you is trying to tell you.
How truly disgusting are the gifts one gives to another's compassion
to be able to buy him off his own logic!

I'm struggling to find a way to convince you
to not let my bankrupt affection cover all the bad checks
given to you by the part of my soul which I always trusted less.
It's the part which my logic lets pass through my body
even though my cunning arguments managed once again
to make the repeated orgasms of your melancholy cheer
without realizing that in a few moments they will cease to exist.

The time has come for me to admit it.
I've become so good at managing to clothe
the demanding accident that once again your hope became today
with that kind of gorgeous, almost mythical
but incredibly unhappy purple compassion,
successfully unlocking from the depths of your being
the delusion I really need right now more than anything
to feel that by defeating my defeatism
I can still feel that I won.

My often duplicitous emotional intelligence
continues to indifferently play with your inability to understand
why I seem like a better person than you could stand me to be.
Strolling for hours undisturbed in those neighborhoods of your mind
you have learned how to defend by now
from the attacks of any meanness except mine,
without realizing what I intend to do,
you let me put two pairs of handcuffs on every hope of yours
and two unanswered questions
on every look you will use in the next few minutes
to feel all that you can no longer understand by just seeing it.
Damn it! Use your eyes to feel and your soul to see!

Why is my damned misery so much more skillful than me?
I quickly left to let you enjoy in the glittering gift I just gave you
the misery of a man who once again
gladly exchanged the most melancholic sample book of his deceit
with the most courageous scream of his own conscience.
It is the conscience that can no longer bend low enough
to gather from the sewer where his own life throws them
those parts of his character
she no longer knows how to hold in her hands
without getting burned herself.
Do you think they are my most impressive good qualities? Maybe.
I will never be able to find out because my hopes just decided
to stop defending the kind of truth
our common future should have long past announced to you
that it's no longer part of the new authenticity
I am launching only to the people I'm trying to convince that I love them.

What is the exchange rate in a transaction between a couple
in which both for different reasons feel obliged every night,
before they refuse to embrace each other,
to embrace the two biggest lies they gave birth to during the day,
lies that demand to not resemble each other at all
so they don't get confused?
When a relationship begins to approach its end
the couple instead of making love to each other
end up with each one making love with his or her favorite delusion
and on the day the relationship actually ends
with his or her favorite lie.
That's why a relationship that doesn't know how to end
furiously searches the last phrases of every fight
trying to find an emergency exit
that will fit not only themselves but their ego too.

And I, trying to keep my body as upright as I can,
while I feel more down on my knees than ever before,
beg you to give me one more chance,
a chance to prove to you how emotionally worthless
but mentally invaluable I am to you.
I beg you, because I know that at some point of your emotional ambiguity
you may still stand to love me,
do not try today to go past the unbearable stench of my shortcomings
to reach the part of my soul where, every time you try to cross it
you end up getting lost.

Another day in which my age and my enthusiasm got into a fight
over which one of the two will shape my day the way it wants!
I feel so happy each time my silence
lets me be the only one she talks to.
At which point in his mind does man place that truth of his
that suddenly fell in love with his biggest delusion?

All that was confided to us by that battle
whose end refused to shield us
from what each one of us thought he won.
Do you know that I get reborn each time I stay true to my beliefs and not my comfort?
What do you think the paradise you've been searching for all these years
at the end of your melancholy knows about you?

You came and left the flavor our life together has acquired lately
on the edge of the one word I could never stand to hear
myself uttering every time we fight.
The day we let our fists sing our favorite song.
Please stop searching in my silence
to find what you wanted to say!

Right now my smile is searching in vain all over me
to find the reason it was born in the wrong mouth.
Perhaps the time has come for me to live for a while in my ego
in hope of finding those arguments
I hid long ago in the most cowardly side of my intelligence.
The prophesy of a vagueness I used years ago
which unfortunately knows more about me than I'd like.

I prick my ears up to hear everything my kisses
are about to confide to your compassion.
Well then, take the tear that the correct operation of my melancholy
asked me to give you as a gift.
I had such a good time casually skating all night
on the surface of your sorrow!

Silence often starts at that point in a conversation
when the stories truth is telling don't know how to end.
We became a couple who in every sunrise
each one sees a different sunset.
Living far longer than I can bear
at the spot in my life where in the heart of August
the first day of winter rushes to hug the end of my soul.

that no longer wish to work for me.

A bit later the first sunbeam of the day finally discovered me and said:
"Please, today don't start making again steps you will never climb."
What I felt when I heard the opinion that the midnight
which tonight refuses to be part of my evening has of me.
Is this the dream I was forced to dream
to be able to get back to my reality?

Dear God, help me quickly construct a fog
so I can escape what I see
each time I start feeling unable to look inside me anymore.
Two sorrows fought with two joys at the edge of your lips
to see which ones would push the first word out of your mouth.
What I felt when for the first time in months
I stopped digging the hole in the middle of my head
in which I would throw my beliefs to drown.

Everything I felt the day I discovered
that my tears still carry with them those deep red words
my joy never let me learn how to pronounce.

that silences live in us long before they are born.
The embraces that never embrace
live in a man for as long as he rushes to hide
the brightest zeros of his life inside his greatest joy
before his sorrow realizes how many they are.

The day that man decides to try to find out
how many zeros in his life he has hidden in his happiness
is the day he will finally manage to liberate himself from his own sorrow.
Am I ready today I wonder to try to find them?
Maybe then I will be able to understand
why when a silence decides to speak
the zeros that were living for years at the edge of its owner's soul
are the ones that speak for it.

My heart's magical dust got drunk
when it realized what I just asked it to hide for me.
One and a half indignation away
my conscience was discovering as time went by
that the darkest room of a house
is the one in which its residents have long hidden any thought of theirs
that has come to fear them more than they fear it.
My crafty conscience, without telling me anything, intends to break into it
hoping this way to make me confess to her
everything I should have told her years ago.
Besides, who said that consciences ever warn their owners
about everything they'll force them to do in the future?

Annoyed by my silence's behavior,
I sat between those two words of mine
which, because they mortally hate each other,
refuse to sit one close to the other
and help me articulate what I need so much to express.
What does my public image do
with all the lies it won't need today
to persuade people to buy me from my very honesty?
Now I understand why my heart was asking me all night yesterday
to find for her all the different kinds of zero
and all the different kinds of rust I have in me,
and then line them all up
so she can figure out which one fits inside another.

I can't tell you how impressed I've always been
by those conversations that only employ words made from broken down glances
and silences made from elderly truths!

So while I was watching my opinion of myself
hanging around the front door of my self-criticism
and not daring to enter,
I observed my authenticity
which, to avoid seeing me flirting with my most charming delusions,
chose to silently remain a reality behind
the one I was experiencing at the time,
waiting for an opportunity to give me a solid push and shove me into it.

You see, after all these years of serving the parts of my logic
that believe more in the quality of life
my ambiguity rather than my self-confidence can offer me,
my poor heart has realized that
to earn the right to choose what color she wants to be,
she must first allow the very rust
I've been covering her with all these years
to sink in deep inside her.

all those character traits of mine I want to hide from myself
so I won't have to realize that they own me more than I own them.

The entire time I wrestled with it
I saw the crescent moon wrestling too with its own light.
It has been doing everything in its powers
to penetrate the shutters of my room
so as to see what's going on inside,
what's happening with a conscience
that is trying to quickly find new ways
to hide what she hasn't found a way yet to discover.

Every minute that went by,
I kept on taking away from the nails of my truth the ability to dig deeply
to try to discover the spot
where I lost my trust in my fellow human beings,
the spot where I lost the ability I once had
to throw the windows of my soul wide open
on the first kind word I would hear
without needing to bring along each time
the iron henchmen of my logic to investigate it in detail
and make it confess what it is really trying to conceal within it.

I think love is when you can trust your partner's silence enough
without feeling the need to cut it into a thousand pieces
to see what it's made of.
When did I start trusting words more than silences?
When did I start trusting the copy more than the original?
When did I start trusting my delusions more than my truth?
At which point in my life, I wonder, did I lose the ability
to simply trust what I feel and not what I see?
I think when, realizing who I could become at any given time,
I stopped trusting my own self,
because when one doesn't trust his own truth any longer
he can't trust anyone else's either.

With this in mind, I started making a cardboard, craven century
out of all the indecent silences I was never able to trust in my life,
and an hour made of yellow rust out of all the distances I kept
from the souls I aggressively stretched my hand out to keep away.

I hid my soul in the back side of the sun
and went into the most half-finished springtime I can make myself
to try to learn how to enjoy my loneliness when I am not alone.

wrapping with the fearless loneliness I felt
one after another the beginning of each of the tens of souls
around which I had endlessly spun all night.
Seconds later, I let those emotions of mine
that have long since stopped trusting me
cut a clear path for me to that spot in my heart
where I am most afraid to go.
It's the spot where for years now
every time I try to feel my next emotion,
I end up accidentally stumbling on my biggest shortcoming
pretending that I don't know it.

I always thought that pessimism is when someone,
regardless what time it is, invites the closest darkness
he can find around at the time to get inside him,
so that night might fall as quickly as possible,
and thus rob him of a chance to find out how much light blue,
how many hopes the sky still has to pull out from inside him
and give them to the day before the end of his shift.
Who knows? Perhaps the end of all that I want to confide
to any color in the sky except light blue
might manage to show me how to be moved again
by realizing how many of his shades I am made of myself.

Why should meannesses be so insatiable?
Feeling that a negative thought just started being born in my innards,
I began hearing in any words of mine
going around my head without having something to do
what the sunset was trying for hours to whisper in my ear.
Unable to do anything to deal with it,
I watched my meanness do all it can
so I won't find where it managed to hide its end
before the sunset locates its own.

Meanwhile, my tears have already started descending from the heavenly sorrows
where they always preferred to live
and chose to go towards my sorrow
rather than any other spot in my life that cannot stand being as real as her.
I am really upset by the fact that the part of my every day routine
that adores my melancholy is always its most real one!

to burn the thousands of asterisks
it had used to hide my delusion behind my honesty
began to look at me with compassion.
These were the asterisks placed in my happiness
by everything in my life which the moment I threw it in the garbage
I knew that someday it could become my most precious possession.

As time went by, the merciful fire
started relaxing its formidable muscles one by one
as if it didn't want to, as if it didn't have any ambition left in it to destroy me.
The light of its flame had managed at that moment to become a worldwide light,
the only light that could illuminate my life
without blinding it, without distorting it.

While its flame kept blazing,
a beautiful heart, an exact copy
of the one I wish I had more than anything in the world,
emerged from what my insecurities always called: "Our ungrateful end"
and came and sat across from me,
at a distance equal to the smallest hope I had at the time in me.
It's the heart which if you lined it up along with a thousand others
it wouldn't take me more than a few seconds
passing in front of it to choose it again.
What a fantastic occasion to find
in the future your dreams dream of on your behalf
those parts of your heart
that have dared to enter it ahead of you.

which I can't even begin to explain
to any other part of myself except my enthusiasm,
just started fighting with the wrong ones,
which I continue to pretend
I do not know the reason I made them.

They are competing about which one will be first
to bring forth from inside it a winner's podium
which they will place right in front of the main gate of my mind,
to bestow awards on those emotions of mine they themselves choose.

Meanwhile, my conscience continues to claim her sun
from the darkest sections of my brain,
and her clouds from the next "thank you"
that's waiting at the edge of my silence
for me to finally let it be born.

The waves my remorse keeps on manufacturing on my behalf
seem to become more bloodthirsty as time goes by,
more determined to swallow up the breakwater my life has built
to protect me from those doubts I have
that I can still stand up to those fragments of myself
which I am ashamed to admit are sadder than me.

These are the moments when a person, armed only with a timid candle,
enters a huge frozen warehouse
where his life has hidden by herself his next decision.
There he will stay for as many hours as it takes for him to decide
which of the dozens of carefully stored suns he sees before him
he will spit in the face and which one he will start believing in.
It is no coincidence that the only emergency exit of my heart
is the only entrance door my next happiness has.

At the corner of this warehouse there is a small tin table
on which I'm forced to empty all the ugliness
my mind has collected through the years without my permission
from everyone and everything beautiful
I was lucky enough to touch in my life.
I am so curious to see, using those exhibits of my ugliness
that still believe a lot in their own future,
how beautiful I can make the next truth I will beget.

The fragments of my soul that I could never let
negotiate without my help their presence in my future
become the frantic guests who arrived unannounced
to entrap me in the most obscure parts of my logic,
parts where every "I will" I uttered
prefers the flavor of every "maybe" I meant to say
from the courage usually displayed by any "probably" I didn't even think of.

I let my anger free, once it has calmed down,
to use any argument it wants to convince me
to pick one of them and love it as much as I can.

I gather speed, divide my body in two
and jump with the biggest part of my weight
and the smallest part of my self-defeatism
inside each of them at the same time,
hoping I will manage to entirely fit
in the lies that my future owes me
before I end up on my knees pleading with my truth
to forgive everything I owe to my past.
I am not sure whether the warped smile of a decision
that is waiting at my mind's front door
to raise me onto the winner's podium it made itself
is more ingenious than guilty,
more dapper than despicable.

Climbing the last step of that podium,
to where the best wrong decision is usually awarded,
I see the most beautiful silky uphill I've seen in my life
pulling down its zipper and hastily stuffing
as many sad but sinful downhills as it can inside it.

Seeing it, I sighed, bowed my head
and, touching the spot in my body
that has forgotten how to manufacture the fire extinguishers
my sorrow needs to extinguish herself,
I slowly started to weave,
from the thousands of small truths in my life
whose true value I always underestimated,
the light I will use to light up my world tomorrow.

in the clouds it should stop fearing.

Pretending you're not affected by the vast emptiness beneath you
you have great difficulty in trying to figure out the value of your next step
which wants to be more uncertain than your courage.
It's time for you to decide on which clouds
you'll pin the two hearts of yours,
and by threading each one with that velvety wire rope
you will start walking on all that you're afraid of
hoping that this way you'll be able to overcome
what you fear even more.

While you're trying as hard as you can
to balance between your most self-confident doubts,
everything your optimism still lets you hope for
will be watching you from the ground with open mouths
waiting for the moment when towards the end of your crossing
you will have proven to yourself
that you respect your hopes more than you fear them.

Your first step just arrived at your leg a minute late,
but full of self-confidence.
The time has come when you'll discover
whether your heart intends to surrender to the self-serving gifts
the clouds that live inside me are bringing her
rather than fall in love again
with the illegal tranquility of our alternate reality,
the one my ego always thought
we deserved to experience together one day.

The time has come for you to realize
that to everything genuine that lives inside you
you owe a lot more than what you think.
Balancing on your least precious darknesses
you'll be able to learn what spring dreams in the middle of winter,
or you'll forget how to let the most important battles of your life
conquer every square inch of the second truth
that your past victories always gave you as a gift
one minute after each time you won.

It is the kind of truth that still believes more in your kindness
than in the tank treads used by
the last optimistic arguments you might have left
to crush the thorns inside the brains of your opponents
that protect their self-confidence from your arrogance.

less than it did in yours.

The memories from the battles you fought
which chose to sell themselves to your darknesses
rather than be forced to buy the light
that your next enthusiasm offered them,
come from all points of the horizon
and empty thousands of little bright yellow bags on your hands.
Inside each little bag there is a promise
your ego gave in the past
to the conscience you were using at that moment.
Any scrupulous sunshine that has the courage to still live
in the part of your logic you control the least
struggles to liberate itself from the obligations you have given it
so it can manage to keep you in balance.

Your hopes just brought and placed
their newly printed user manuals
two thirds of the distance between your two hearts.
Still suspended, you sense the two clouds in front of you
and the one just behind you
slowly hugging their reason for living,
daring your truth to wrap her hand around your neck
and start to squeeze with all her strength.
Tomorrow no longer asks you for more hollow guarantees.
The self-taught pages of your autobiography
don't seek out that strangely inconsistent company
your logic always offered them.

You start being afraid because you don't know what to fear.
You start being afraid because you can't feel
in which part of the rest of the day
is your most precious sorrow located.
You hear the last hope you have in your mind right then
reading out loud the three questions she always wanted to ask you
knowing that you only have two answers in you to give her.

While you still continue to walk on the tightrope,
you feel as if your own intelligence
has set personal traps in its section you can't clearly see,
which, knowing that they won't be able to catch anybody else except you,
seek to find a way to hide in your lungs
before you take your next breath.

Dumbfounded, you see your ego bent over counting one by one the rewards
your character strengths will soon start offering it to let you pass.
There, between your next step and your next thought,
if you actually manage to convince your courage to finally think it,
will grow the future you always wanted to have.
As long as you try to balance yourself
while walking on the edge of your time
you will see slowly emerging from the middle of your previous step
the past you always wanted to avoid.

The eyes that your arrogance recently gave you free of charge
close as tightly as they can,
believing that if they can't see
they might possibly be able to understand.
The time has finally come for you to find out after all these years
who the proud manufacturer of your sorrow is.

I probably should try to find inside me
the first sunbeam that will help me understand
where it derives its power so I can defeat it.
Instead of complaining about what I cannot see
I probably should try to understand what I can already see.
When will I finally realize that a fog always hides
the reason it was born a second before it reveals its end?

You think I might be able now to figure out
why I've been endlessly wandering for days
around the few things I can still understand
without considering it necessary to have already touched them with my mind?
Perhaps this is the bit of knowledge
that could give me the strength to toss into the trash
the next step of mine that wants to first teach me how to retreat
before I convince it to move forward.
This way I might free my cowardice
from the promises it made to my defeatism
even though I can't clearly make out
the favors my next step is already asking of me.

I live almost constantly embracing uncertainty.
I live almost constantly embracing the uncertainty
of not knowing how I should feel
about the moments of my life I have intentionally left emotionally vacant,
the ones during which I indifferently stare at my own emotions overtaking me,
choosing to go try other hearts first
which might be able to feel them.

I have to face it.
I now live in the company of that favorite fog of mine
which every morning weaves for me three versions of today,
one made from a piece of iron,
one from uncertainty and one from honesty,
the honesty the first two give birth to
each time I ask them to tell me what they want from me.
If these three weren't part of my life
then everything would be crystal clear,
maybe then I wouldn't need at the end of every fight with my own ego
to rush off to have time to recreate from scratch
the secret life of my biggest delusion
before my self-criticism manages to figure out what's happening.

Why is man always so eager to sell to his melancholy
the part of his happiness he needs most of all?
It's probably that uncertainty he feels
when he comes to believe that he no longer owes anything to his own honesty,
when he realizes that he is no longer afraid of her

I wonder, do I have the right to ask the one I love
to lend me the fog in which she herself lives
because it's no longer enough for me to hide only in mine?
Against the advice my past never stops shouting at me to stop trying to get across,
I keep on building that bridge because, like most people,
every morning in my life that finds the courage
to not fear the optimism of the sun that illuminates it,
I end up deciding to leave the side of the river I am at,
to abandon certainty and the incredible warmth I feel
each time "zero" decides to embrace me
so I can try to get across to the uncertainty of "one".

The danger is fascinating but unknown, beyond measure,
and even more unknown is the victory that supposedly awaits me on the other side.
I leave behind me the slightly abused comfort
I have secured for the part of my life
that refuses to contain sweat and tight wooden chairs,
only laziness and comfortable sofas,
and begin to build a bridge using as construction materials
the optimism I found while looking through my most daydreaming footsteps
trying to find out where my beginning is.
These are the steps I often forget
out what kind of dreams I made them from in the past,
perhaps those dreams that were ready to instantly love my future
more than they ever loved me.
So I end up letting each one place on my behalf
one more bet with the fog that lives inside me,
a fog that prefers to live in locked answers
rather than freewheeling questions.

Walking on that bridge I turn my head from time to time
and watch all the "zeros" I loved in my life
which have lied down on one of those beautiful, comfortable sofas
and have happily fallen asleep on top of each other.
Hearing the polyphony of choices
the insecurity I feel just then wants to make,
I keep on moving believing that some of my thoughts
will soon refuse to follow me.

They only let me talk with the fog,
they only let me live with the apology I owe my success,
they only let me dance with the words I owe
to that discussion one has when speaking with someone
he soon realizes that the real answers
to the questions he asks the person he is talking to
will later be provided by his own self.
These are the singular moments
when the dialogue will decide to stop by itself,

I allowed my words to sell what I never managed to make mine.
Looking at all those words watching me
to see when they'll start celebrating
once I finally manage to reach the opposite bank
and when they'll start celebrating even more if I fail,
I end up hearing just an appalling monotonous but cyclical sound.
It's the sound that contains that version of me
which my shortcomings fear most of all,
a sound that keeps on insistently asking my heart
to make for me using the biggest doubts she has in her
a cowardice that's even less courageous than mine.

While the guaranteed solutions have gathered around me idly chattering,
every "zero" that loved me in my life
doesn't stop making fun of any "one" that ignored me,
whoever is lying down doesn't stop mocking whoever is still standing,
whoever refuses to be honest
doesn't stop laughing at the one who is still conscientious.
But I'm not giving up.
I move on because I'm still fascinated by the love stories
my enthusiasm used to tell me every night
during which, because I was afraid to stay alone with my ambiguity,
I ran as fast as I could to curl up in an embrace.
It was the embrace which had been secretly made
by both my loneliness and its favorite paradise
at the edge of the only reality in my life
I couldn't understand why it didn't belong to me already.
You see, man likes to live at the edge of his reality
because there he can hang out free of charge
with the various excuses he uses
to evade the questions he sooner or later has to ask his true potential.

There, in the middle of the icy bridge,
I stayed for hours hearing the mesmerizing song
of the sirens of convenience calling me back
and the eerie sound produced
by the clenching and unclenching jaws of the voracious waves below me
that were carefully generated by every lie I ever told
which demanded to cause more trouble in the life of the people around me
than it did in mine.
These suspicious, angry waters leaped right at me, trying to swallow me,
to make me pay the price for who I became from time to time
while trying to avoid defending who I actually was.
Doing all I could to not disappoint my disappointment even more,
I focused on the distant echo of my ego's applause
I heard coming from across the bridge and kept on moving.

I moved on without being able to hear clearly
the explanations my next footstep was asking of me,

I had never managed to come into contact with.

After some agonizing seconds I managed to grasp in my palm
everything I couldn't touch with my mind.
My soul was afraid to order my fingers to unclench,
but ignoring her, they relaxed and slowly managed it.
When they opened up completely, the only thing I found
lying in the middle of my palm were some grains of deep red soil.
I looked at them bewildered and, because I couldn't understand what I felt,
I began to forcefully rub them on my face
until I realized that somehow, inexplicably, this was dirt I already knew.
I knew it well because it was the soil I had repeatedly stepped on,
not to move ahead, but to dirty it.

It seems that whatever I've managed to achieve in my life
I did it by finding a way to get through the fog,
not the one I saw before me,
but the one I felt when I pretended not to look inside me.

five or six words anxiously shoving each other
trying to come up from deep inside me
vying for which one will reach my mouth first.

Each one wants more than anything
to get a chance to believe in the meaning it carries within it
before malice, which runs faster than all of them, reaches my lips first,
thus managing to throw the others violently out of their own meaning
just to prove to the people around me
how much stronger than any of my other emotions she is.

Just beyond, the dominance sought by the image
I casually serve to those clients of my logic
who don't know how to correctly buy what I'm not trying to sell,
is looking for a pretext to quarrel
with the least optimistic section of my intelligence.

To survive I continue, without stopping even for a second,
to wrap the tempest of the cardboard apology
around the most stainless phrases I can find waiting for me in my mind
hoping I'll manage to convince some of the most fanatic supporters
of my deadlocked hypocrisy to come back and start worshipping me again.

After successfully neutralizing the unbelievably strong probing rays
the flashlights of their logic shine upon me,
I hope to manage to falsify the result
before I'm forced to act as the cynical interpreter
between what I feel and what I show that I feel.

The part of my reality that still wishes to remain invisible to me,
because of the many dangerous maneuvers I asked it to make on my behalf,
eventually got completely disoriented
and, disappointed, surrendered to the neon sign
located in the middle of my forehead,
which for hours has been trying unsuccessfully to turn itself on.
My gaze is almost ready to stop asking me daily
to start explaining to it who I try so hard to become.

Once more I was able, by trapping your heartbeat
in the arrogant certainty of my own downfall,
to shove myself in the first room I found
which had somewhat less than four walls around it.

the new spelling my soul uses
to explain all that is not happening to me.

I grabbed the most impatient darkness I could find,
pinned it on my forehead
and closed my eyes hoping to convince it
to try to steal for me all that I wasn't able to steal from it.

to illuminate a single square inch of her own surface,
withdrew hours ago from the celestial stage
and is trying to sleep in the bed
which the few stars still loyal to her made a little while ago.

Close to her intend to squeeze those doubts of mine
which will stay up all night to make sure that by morning
they will have learned how to not insult
any white part of my soul
that still has the courage to belong to me.

Half a universe away,
the sun, tightly secured to its most arrogant forces,
begins again to dominate the frailties of all the underlings it illuminates.
Its fiery dialogues with any part of my intellectual nudity
that dares even momentarily to look straight at it,
applaud the touch of the rays it sends onto any flaw of mine
which is still struggling to find a way to awaken me
from the sleep that my melancholy has put me in.

It is these precious morning sunbeams
that I want to convince my soul to absorb one by one
hoping they'll help me figure out how to demystify
the inadequacy I'm almost certain that I will feel during the day.
As soon as those rays see me,
they will ask me to allow them to get inside me
to uproot from the most profound spot they can reach
the greed felt by my mind's most secret hope,
that I can start putting together a tomorrow
by using only materials inside my head
that are compatible with my comfort.

Do I have time, I wonder, to seek a truce
with all that my truth is afraid of?
Do I have time, I wonder, to decommission the happiness of my fears
before I have to stand up and face
the huge yellow and red steamroller of my self-knowledge
that's slowly, yet majestically coming straight at me?
Will I have time, I wonder,
during one more deranged exhibition of my tolerances
to convince my fears to impregnate any courage I still have left
with any truth it produced for my benefit?

Thankfully dusk came just in time
and stole the weight of proof from me.
It came to liberate me from the shackles of my facade
which keeps refusing to accept the downpayment I'm giving it
for the services it so cheerfully provides me with.

Seconds later I see my authenticity rip out from inside me
all the iron bars that belong to it
and carry them out of my body
so they can herald to the entire world
my greatest weaknesses one by one.
The different kinds of my favorite guilt
once again succeeded in putting me to sleep
before I had time to realize how many they were.

Unable to do otherwise
my soul locked herself again in her handmade castle,
which is illuminated day and night
by the most colorless darknesses
she found lying next to my beliefs,
while she simultaneously managed to convince all the stars in the sky
to fall asleep before my naiveté asked me
to introduce them one by one to it.
Just as well, because if I could understand
any more of what is happening to me,
I would be a lot more miserable.

listening to the horrible sounds its end is emitting from afar.
Holding in my right hand
the white towel I am ready to throw at my greatest joy,
I feel my body, for the first time after many years,
stop spinning around the core of my fears
and ask me to let it walk even for a little while
a few inches in front of me.

My feet decide on their own
to sink into the hundreds of reticent questions
the crimson dead end that I see in front of me asks me,
but I don't allow them to.
Discovering that my soul's arms still have some strength left in them,
I decide for the first time in my life
to leave unpaid the monthly bill
my fears keep on sending to my optimism.

From within the thoughts which at that moment
arise from every truth around me
that isn't dancing with its favorite lie
I see new words coming out of my mouth,
words which I never knew that someday would allow me to use them.

They anxiously rush to immediately deactivate
anything black they see in my life
before they start believing in any other color.
I don't despair over any strength
that I feel in these moments inside me which I am willing to betray,
only over any strength of mine I can't fully believe in.

I am ready to believe before I understand.
I am ready to go to battle before I believe.

Surrounded by thousands of emotions I haven't felt in years,
for some reason I can't explain, I feel that I am completely alone.
I let my soul's strength flow freely out of my body
and spill on the ground which for the first time in months
I sense that it is not standing on me,
I am standing on it.
The poor thing stayed awake all night waiting up for me
so that by morning I would have learned
how to understand what the endless stillness it hides inside it wants to say to me.

I see the sky having lit thousands of torches inside its own body
to show me where to go.
I don't need them.
I no longer need anybody's light to see what I want to feel.
I am so pleased to finally be able to understand
that every beginning starts off inside a darkness
that doesn't know yet how to give birth to an end.

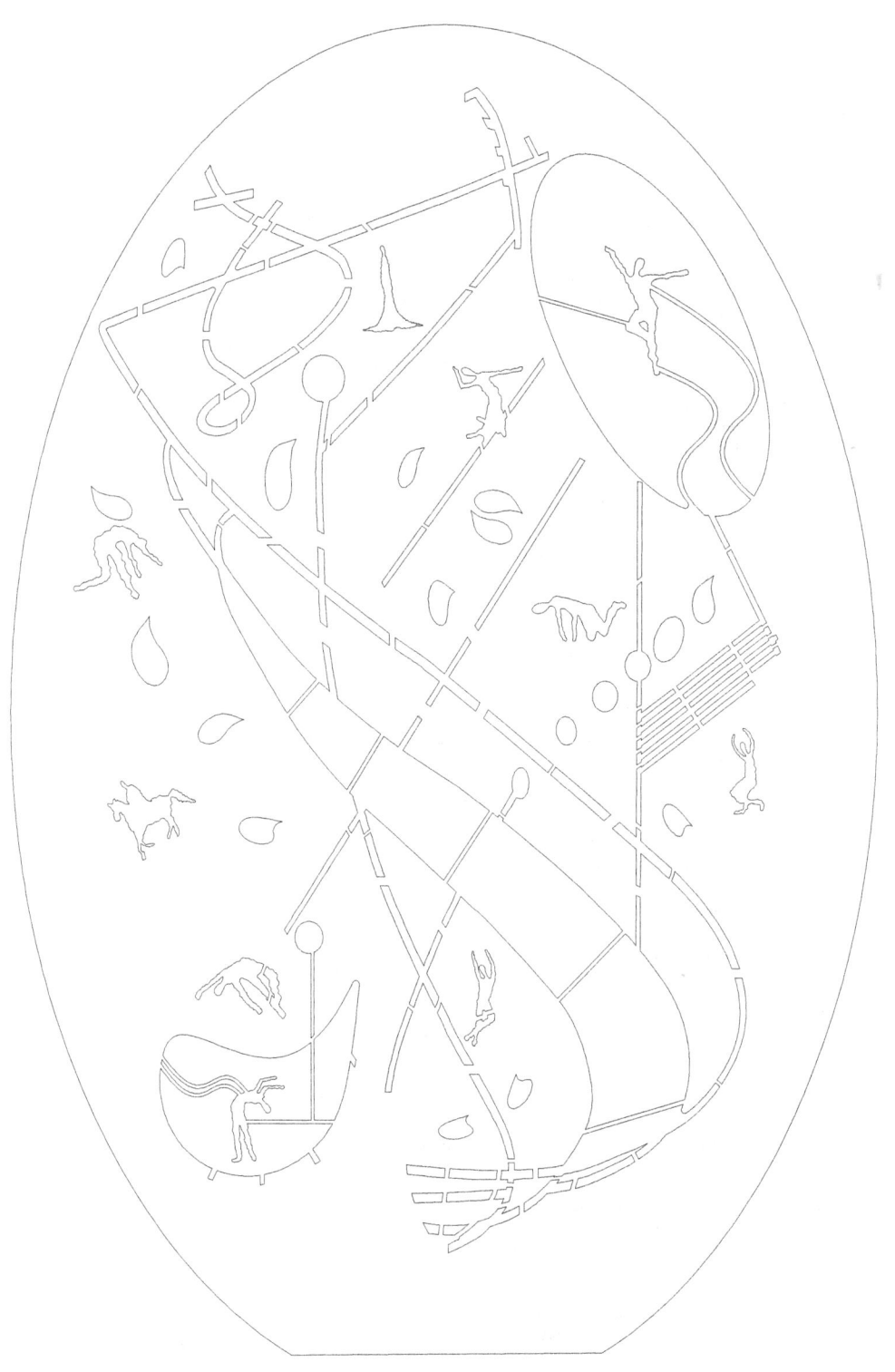

or distinguish less well the bright spots of my triumphs?

While drinking my victories one after the other
in the amorphous glass just offered me
by the huge billboard in the center of my brain,
I thirsted for more explanations from them.

A bit later the main avenue of my mind came in front of me
and threatened to turn itself into a rough dirt road.
Feeling the heavy tread of my flaws
on the most sensitive section of my heart,
I let my victories free to express themselves in any way they wanted,
and the first thing they did
was to surround themselves with a thick barbed wire
that, once installed, is visible to everyone except them.

I sat for hours leaning my back
on the questions I'm afraid to ask my latest victory,
hearing her breathing heavily while trying to carry
an enormous load from her front side to the rear,
where that giant warehouse is located
in which she stores all those sorrows of mine
that know how to give birth,
without the slightest help from me, to more sorrows.

I wanted, if only for a short while, to be able to hide behind her back,
to flee the bright lights that shone on her.
I wanted to feel as much of a winner as I really am,
naked beside the blurriness of the two-headed triumph,
freed from the absurd lies my scheming victory feeds me
just to keep me at the highest spot on the podium
where my self-confidence is ready to hand me my medal.

I wanted to feel real,
not decorated like a Christmas store display,
wearing the shinning attire that suits the image of a winner
who has yet to figure out why he feels so compelled to keep on winning
wars which he never had to fight in the first place.

It's during these wonderfully hollow moments,
realizing that I don't need the applause of my ego to survive,
that I curl up inside the most welcoming part of my embrace
waiting for everything I have achieved in my life
to come to me and press their bodies right next to my own
and start hugging me with all the compassion I don't have any more.

I don't have to go
neither to the left nor to the right, neither higher nor lower.
I am exactly where I want to be.
Tomorrow no longer breathes faster than me.
Tomorrow no longer sees dreams which are more beautiful than mine.
The end of each day of my life
from now on has decided to coincide
with the start of the next one.

in the rhythm that she sets,
my boat doggedly pushes them back
like two good friends joking with each other
verbally pushing one another,
without realizing though that each one is loading every word of his
with different doses of play and competition.

Every so often, throwing me a few handfuls
of the magical blue meadows that live inside her,
urging them to spread as quickly as they can around my body
and embrace me with each one's different soul,
she makes me feel as if I am bigger than my smallest hatred
and smaller than my biggest virtue.

When I reach the island,
and I am finally able to come close to her
I feel that, before I even touch her,
she has already managed to go past my normality
and instantly dive inside me.
By letting her grab the clothes
the next step of my life has put on me, and throw them off me
I hand over to her whatever has made me feel more sad than serene,
whatever has made me feel more like a scrawny pigeon than a proud eagle.

Taking my sorrow from the hands of my soul
and carefully installing it in her embrace,
letting my body slip into hers,
she plunges me into the optimism contained
in the play of every wave of hers, every child of hers.
Raising me a few moments later to the surface of my life,
she makes me feel more real and less of who I really am,
an ordinary pickpocket of those questions
which my wounded self-confidence
doesn't stop asking the most mistreated part of the meaning of my life
in front of my panicked serenity.

Each time I leave my body in the embrace of the sea
I feel an incredible game between the pebbles she herself installed in my soul
and her magnanimous caress unfurling from inside me.
She has the ability with her enormous yet so tender memory
to play with them sending each time a different ripple
to overturn them, to caress them,
and sometimes even to slightly frighten them,
reminding them of the incredibly massive,
yet transparent strength she has.

but that I can stand not knowing what is hidden behind them.

I am afraid they contain
all those raging from the black storm moments of my life
which at the end of each argument with my own self
I ended up dumping into her out of sheer frustration
because I couldn't stand letting the toxic truth
that lived inside me touch me.
She took all those moments in her hands
and immediately stored them together
with the ones I had previously thrown in
because she knew that the day would come
when I would go down on my knees and plead with her
to bring me face to face with them again.

Today I pass by them ignoring them
pretending I don't see them,
trying not to think of the tremendous amount of sorrow,
the thousands of fake precipices I have thrown inside them
so I can easier convince myself
that my life has more straight lines than curves,
more highways than dirt roads.

It's amazing with what incredible ease the sea can poke
her powerful arms into the depths of my soul
and start pulling those doorways one by one out of me.
Spreading them gently on the surface of my life,
she starts opening them one at a time
and, after welcoming everything they hid for all those years behind them,
the reasons that insist on making me suffer,
she introduces them to me one after the other
explaining to me what each one wants from me.

She takes them for a few seconds inside her
and she returns them a few minutes later,
less abrupt, less toxic, less ambitious.
After all, she is the one who taught me
that whoever doesn't manage to kiss his sorrow on the mouth
ends up living in a never-ending twilight
which consists of small invisible handmade ambiguities,
ambiguities which are individually fashioned
out of the trash that his soul throws in the face of each hour of his life
he does not know what to do in order to enjoy it.

to drain the black out of every darknesses
till she makes it look less ambitious,
less sharp, less willing to hurt.

Man always knew how to hide a piece of himself,
probably his most sensitive one,
in the spot of the sea that he believed was emotionally nearest to him.
He handed it over to her
because he knew that he could not withstand
keeping it constantly on him,
not only because it was incredibly valuable
but because it was also extremely toxic.

I want to learn all that the sea has to teach me.
I want to learn to live like she does,
to live a life which won't adhere to any rule
except for her happiness,
because out of a soul you can make a sea
and out of a sea, a serenity.

the first minutes of his own downfall.
Same with me.
The flavor of a defeat that no one else but me can see
as time goes by, becomes more attractively toxic,
but more silently bloody.

Now I realize that all these years I grew up together
with all that I hesitated to fear.
What a shame!
While the last optimism that was left with me on consignment
by the least self-serving color of my sorrow
continues to craft the questions I had left unanswered from yesterday,
I decide to leave today alone to grow up without any of my advice.

With the help of my most belligerent weakness
I transformed myself into the second page of my own ambition,
and the third of my catharsis,
where the triumph of a sorrow that never wanted to have a face
is grateful for the sweat that needed to flow for it to be born.
It is also in those two pages
that time always learned how to memorize
even the least important despair of its owner
so it can recite it to him anytime the magnificent black
asked him to get up on the central stage of his life
so it could show him the great magic tricks
it could perform with the help of his soul.

Unable to lay claim to the rest of my day
from the flawlessly stupid questions
I can't stop asking tomorrow,
I feel that all the great ideas in my life
that always refused to understand me
have already started cutting up my logic into countless little pieces.
They intend to scatter them as far away from me as they can
so I could never gather them, stick them back together
and thus give me another chance to try to understand them.

They pass at astronomical speeds conspicuously close to my silence
convincing my tears to refuse to introduce themselves to my truth
which has already started to flow alongside them on my cheeks.
She wants so much to carve with her toxic substance
a moat between the shadows of the first silence
that wants to rush into my mouth to save me from myself
and the second sad excuse that is willing to exit from it
to save me from my misery.

Sorrow of mine, please show me all that I still can't understand,
make me feel again the reasons I once fell in love with my happiness.
My future today has decided not to question its correct dosage.
Sorrow of mine, would you be kind enough
to teach me from the beginning how to cry?

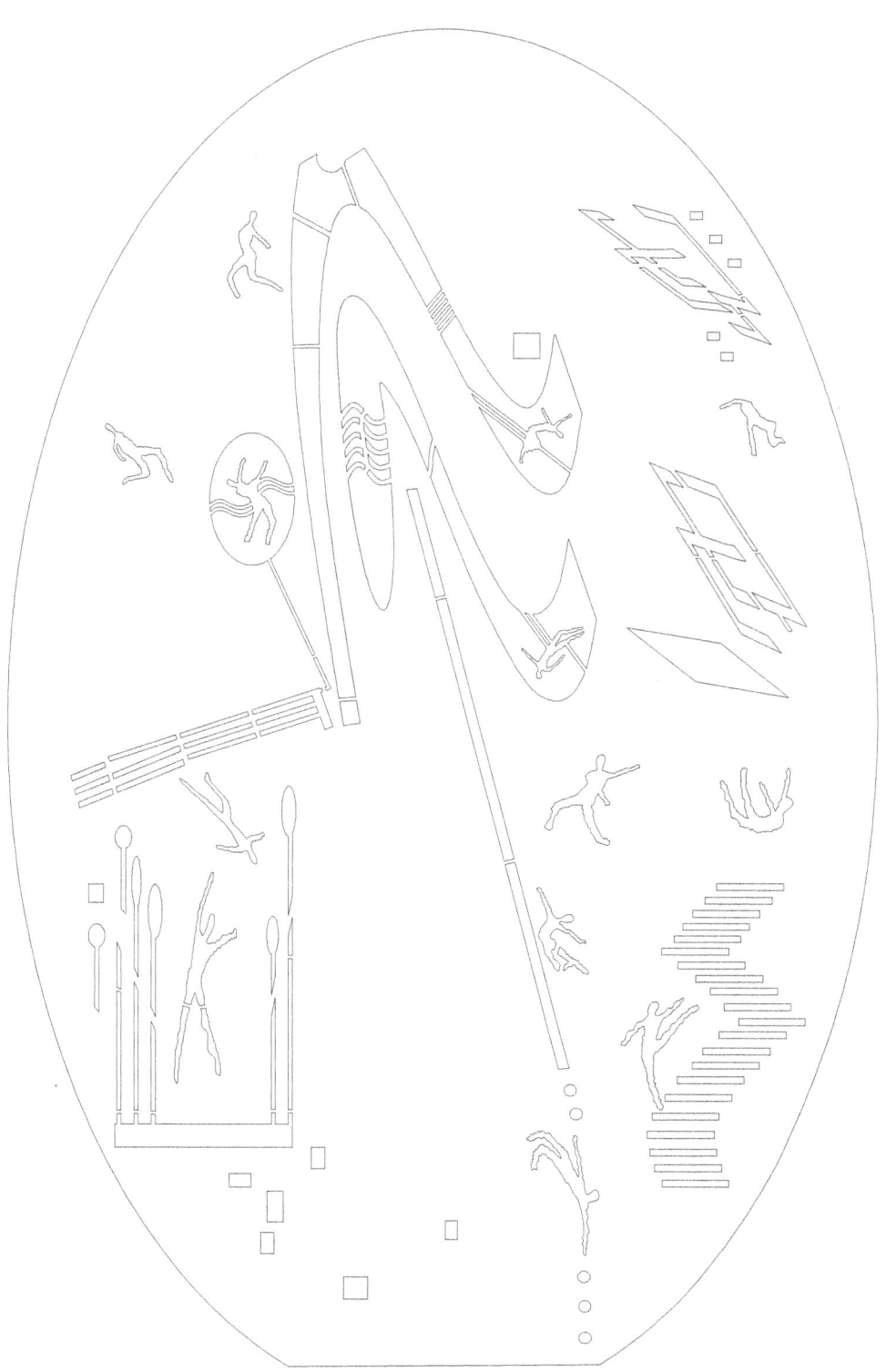

at least once a week in front of her own phobias
just to prove to myself that I'm more powerful than her.

I am ready to concede that the sole owner
of the tempest I encounter every morning
standing in front of my mirror looking at itself
is my own identity.
Trying to push it away from the mirror
hoping I'll get a chance to look at myself,
I opened the half-closed door of my phobias
and entered the dizzying mistake
that patiently awaits me on the back side of the mirror since yesterday
to show me how many different steering wheels
are simultaneously driving my life.

How can a soul, though, fit in a mistake she has not committed herself?
I don't know and, to tell you the truth,
I'm struggling with all the mental strength I have
to avoid finding out today.
I am afraid, however, that she can
if the conscience of her owner has learned from an early age
to pretend that she can't hear the truth which shouts at her
from the deepest part of that gloomy, long and narrow arcade she built
so she could hide all those thoughts
she never learned how to sell.

It's me that's telling you this,
the man who hates his authenticity
more than his own lies,
the man who lay his last betrayed dreams
on the next step of the ladder he has promised his arrogance
to do everything necessary in order to climb.
Don't forget that I always considered fake
the genuine signature of the soul
I was creating every morning from scratch
to justify the mistakes of the previous one,
letting the fakery of any fragile serenity I felt inside me
concoct the individual flavor of each new day.

My authenticity came today accompanied by all its footnotes,
except the ones I've written myself.
My beliefs did manage to carry for yet one more time with them
the burly asterisks that had since late afternoon dozed off
among my least successful lies.
Great! I just saw my vanity gleefully continuing to leave before my feet
new stair steps for me to climb.

conducted by my cowardice through those dreams of mine
which I don't seem to be able to convince the night to let me dream,
I lay outstretched on the shadow
my body was painting on the surface of those questions
I wouldn't dare ask myself right then.

I tried to apply the limits of my body,
a body that was never interested in learning how to remember,
only how to forget,
as closely as I could on the outline of my shadow,
hoping I'll find even for a short while some protection from my own light
which more than anything is trying to find even more painful ways to blind me.

I sat for hours aimlessly next to the comfortable questions
my shadow kept asking me with great gusto,
unable to get through the velvet wall
that the meaning of my life so generously constructed for me.

The fog of a memory struggling to free itself
from the guilt it creates for the benefit of its owner
gets tangled up in the purity of what I feel
the moment I try as hard as I can to find new ways
to protect the end of my memory
from the begging of my innocence.

Touching the invisible missteps
that are agonizingly dripping from the memories
I'm doing my best to not understand what they want me to remember,
I am trying to fit the most square sorrow I've seen in my life
into the perfectly round interpretation of my own happiness.

I gathered around me as hastily as I could
all the mistakes that have long chosen to live in my memories
so I wouldn't have time to feel the tremendous effort they are making
to suck me back to the part of my past
I am not certain I experienced.
The little buggers are struggling to wrap themselves around my hopes
to immobilize them in their non-negotiable rust
and maybe manage this way to convince them
not to pull out from inside them any more future for me.

In the involuntary middle of this image
I was able to finally liberate, not only my agony from my logic,
but the dreams of one from the nightmares of the other.
Wrapped in the abundance of fears that no longer fascinate me
but also in the profusion of those joys that still feel sorry for me,
I disguised myself as my most self-destructive escape
and jumped along with every last ounce of my body
into the part of my past where anxiously awaiting me for hours
was a sweet remembrance which long ago decided
to never cross the entrance of my memory.

Why did you let me become the lock you use at the end of each day
to lock up your heart inside my anger? Why?
The moment a person exchanges a signature with a conscience
is the same as the one he sells yet another truth of his
to his favorite dead end.

Listening to my next thought
curse at what's left of my cowardice once I manage to take out of it
all the dreams my self-confidence has for me.
Tell me, at what point in our relationship was the gain of an illusion
not the loss of a truth?
What I learned about myself
by touching the foundations of every emotion
I managed to feel for the first time in my life.

The part of tomorrow that never believed in the assurances
I gave it that I will become a better person.
Did you know that the last organ of the human body
that could discover this kind of lie is the ear?
This must probably be the joyful constraint
a past imposes on a sorrow so it won't feel even sadder.

What I learned from the version of myself
that refuses to be the one I will don in the next few minutes.
Listening to the global radio station of happiness
invite everyone around me except me.
Come on, big winner! The time has come for you to conquer,
the time has come for you to feel even lonelier than the trophy you are about to win.

While we were talking, you never stopped taking out of the pockets of your heart
one giant seawall after another to try to break the waves of my sorrow.
Listening to my wear and tear talking to you about me.
The part of the night my hopes will keep dragging behind them
until they come across the day's first sunbeam
that will believe more in my kindness than in my strength.

Every stupidity of mine knows how to quickly hide
what the back side of my intelligence just said.
Whoever I refused to hate in my life
came after many years before me,
took a step back and told me that he likes me.
I wore the angriest side of my logic next to my skin
and rushed out to calm down my anxiety.

without having to carry my biggest sorrow with me.
Man is freed from the promises he has made to his cowardice
the moment he starts demolishing the limitations
his greatest delusions have built around him.

In the next few minutes the sunset
will choose from among the people who pretend they don't see it
its new teammates and its new opponents.
I just discovered that I no longer know how to hide
in between the hiding places my courage constructed
so it won't reveal me to the weakest parts of my brain.
My honesty can find no other argument in my logic
to persuade me to tell it no more lies.

All those awkward emotions I felt
while holding in my hands the two small fragments of my cry
that never wished to frighten me.
"Go right through me" my next decision sweetly nodded to me
when it saw me sinking in self-doubt.
Who wants to permanently live one floor below his inferiority?

Who knows? Maybe this is the moment
when all the brave silences of my life
decide to demand an explanation from my wrong decisions.
I can no longer break the code
my heart uses to understand what I'm saying to her.
The part of my logic that taught me
how to hit people without hurting myself.

Are you ready to sell all those pieces of yourself
that your palm can no longer bear to hold in it
to the next person you will shake hands with?
Happy is the person who knows
how to protect his self-awareness
from what his mirror wants to do to it.
Your erotic caresses always preferred to leave
at the spot where my dignity borders my body
messages that have sold their meaning to my insecurities.

Now I understand why sorrow is the only profit of a successful loneliness.

are knocking on my door already.
Please tell me. Is this the way a wound teaches its owner how to hurt?
Quickly looking to find how many truths
which until today I thought were lies
are hidden in a night that's afraid to show its naked body
before the last light of the day fades out.

The internal monologue of a laugh
that forgot almost from the beginning of the conversation
the reason I have asked it to lie.
An old silence once told me: "Stop talking and let me look into your eyes
so I can figure out what you are trying to tell me."
The tears of a silence dry only on words
that have not yet learned how to express their owner's pain.

The scenarios written by my wear and tear on the side of my injury
that no longer remembers how to heal
without the help of my worst pain.
My whole life is written on the back side of an old eraser
I used to erase my mistakes off the end of every day.
Perhaps this is the lifetime role of a thought
that never wanted to play the lead role in its owner's happiness.

Let's convince this day to use only comas,
no full stops.
The fake relief I felt the moment I surrendered to my ambiguity
so I can let it mold me anyway it wants.
Filling to the brim my personal abyss
with horizons that no longer believe in the sky they represent.

Believe me, I've been doing my best
to no longer be my ambition's only product.
Letting myself be absorbed by the end of a smile
that for hours now has been carrying on my behalf
all that I don't want to tell you.
The part of myself I met
going up the stairs to the next decision
my future made without asking me.

This is probably what a writer feels
watching the moves of his shadow
while it is dancing alone on top of every word he is writing
trying to describe to his pencil
everything his soul confided to him.
The part of a conversation where only defective silences bloom.
Right next to it you can see the part of my life
where rugged truths that would give anything to be lazy lies live.

I just confided to you what I feel
when I touch with the edge of my soul the different landscapes I see inside me
each time I catch myself
the moment I try not to seem like I'm looking into the mirror
in front of which supposedly I've been standing unintentionally for hours.

to rip out the part of my identity
I pretend that I don't hide there.
It's as if it does all it can to keep me
several steps behind my own growth,
several dreams behind my submission to reality.

Today I feel the darkness of my own luck
glowing inside me brighter than ever.
It seems that the ambiguity of what is random and what is not
no longer needs my help
to defeat the most outward limits of my optimism.
It's been trying since this morning to convince me
to lose all those insecurities I'm sure I don't feel
so I can try to regain the self-confidence
I never was sure was absolutely mine.

Surrounded by that tiny serenity inside me
in which my luck met for the first time in my life its own sadness,
I kick as hard as I can all those parts of me
that still insist on proving my innocence,
start blaming any victory I achieved
using borrowed muscle and borrowed luster
and begin to march by using the decisive steps I have in me
to the one tiny spot inside me
where I think my greatest insecurities always came from.
I wonder, can I really appreciate the amount of joy that my success brings me
more than the quantity of self-knowledge
my heaviest defeats love to drag continuously behind me?

I am not sure.
Truth refuses to give birth to the interpretations of my life I ask her to.
Entangled in those uncompromising light-blue ambiguities
I helped my ego tie around my neck
and taking my time's greed by the hand,
I embrace every darkness that chose to live inside my luck instead of inside me
and every next step of my self-confidence that has already betrayed me
before even trying to believe in me.

What luck fears most of all is its own abundance.
Thus I'm trying, not only to live a life
balancing on the limits of my most primitive agony,
but also to learn new ways to enjoy her.

This is the hope that waits for me to wake up every morning
to explain to me what that sparkling echo has been trying for some time to tell me,
the one left behind by randomness
every time it passes through the center of my life
without getting injured.
Grabbing that exact randomness in my hand
I began cutting that echo in as many pieces as I could
until I started feeling more confident about who I am not.

Another small victory, another small sunbeam
I hope that lives somewhere between those greedy canyons of my luck
that never miss an opportunity
to parade a few inches from my face
the dead bodies of the capabilities I once had,
the ones they themselves massacred with such joy.

I walked for hours on the favorite beach inside my heart,
hand in hand with my own breath
until I was able to understand it.
Spring today forgot its most cherished day
on the lowest step of my soul.

my erotic facade had made till then to everybody I tried to love.
Two of those thieving emotions of mine
again didn't pay the bill my sorrow brought you.
The way today's lover
chooses to become the enemy of tomorrow's love.

Faced with your smile, the victory of my malice misplaced its beginning.
I just started paying my soul's bill in installments
from those ruins of mine that pretend they no longer recognize each other.
Grasping in my hands all the unprocessed words my heart contains at this moment
I am trying to write a letter to the emotion
I felt the moment I met you.

I don't know if I saw right, but ten answers
that don't know in whose ears to end up
just brushed past what you just asked me.
Are you sure you can fit to pass in between your beauty
and those tears of hers that flow out of your eyes
when you look into her mirror?
What I hear living a whisper away
from the loudest zero I have ever heard in my life.

The mud got off the ground and ran after me
to catch me and befoul me as much as it could
with the same questions I asked my beauty a while ago
when I froze looking at the reflection of myself in a street pothole.
The applause of a serenity my melancholy chose never to hear.
What I learned living a landfill away
from the person I chose to become.

The last page of a love that never wanted to know
what the first one has been yelling at it.
I wrapped any minute of my life that didn't know how to feel
with those fugitive adolescent questions that chose to briefly lend
their interpretation to law-abiding middle-aged qualms.
Come on now, you know that either way I can no longer fit
in any old truth that wants to become part of my new self-awareness.

How I detest the grand but bankrupt parades my fears organize
to impress my self-esteem!
Trying to count how many imperfect dreams I still have in me
I ended up counting the number of heavily used "maybes"
the biggest part of my normal dimensions is made of.
Every person cultivates in him
orchards where curses flourish
and landfills where the warmest embraces bloom.

Please let me borrow an old friend of mine from your heart,
an emotion of mine I left with you to look after
at a time when I had no idea what to do to try to feel it.
I can no longer be in love with the only photocopy of my happiness
which when I place it right next to you
makes me seem like I'm made of only two colors,
black and blacker.
Why did every word that came out of our mouths
while we were talking about our future
increasingly become invisibly ambitious?

A bed full of evening ulterior motives
is a good-morning that even before daybreak
has managed to drain itself of all its substance.

and the brightest part of your mind?
I haven't!
I feel that each one of these words carries so much pain in it,
enough to alter the slightly downhill course
my day has started following on its own
before I even begin to weigh it down with my own worries
till it becomes extremely dangerous.

Seeing myself trying to feel
before I'm forced to start thinking
so that I can solve the next problem I see taking shape
on reality's border with my stupidity,
I wonder why the hundreds of tiny teachers
that usually live in the better organized part of my mind
today decided to come out all at once
appearing one by one out of that cloud
my most insistent cowardice has leased
from my huskiest ambiguity.
They want so much to persuade me to not take the next step
unless I first make sure that the foot I will use
is securely bolted first to my courage
and then to my body.

I have so much to tell you, though,
because I have so many shackles to break.
Maybe more than I even knew I have in me
since I have to free myself from so many darknesses.
How nice it is to see an emotion
that was never sure it could stand living inside you
suddenly come straight at you asking to meet you!

I always knew how to sit.
Now the time has come for me to prove to myself
that I also know how to stand up.
I'm tired of always kissing on the mouth those darknesses
that for years were the only ones that kept company
with the part of my loneliness that never wanted to leave me alone.
So I decided to no longer obey
the totally free of charge misery
which all the "maybes" I uttered the previous day
so generously insist on leaving for me
at daybreak on the remotest part of the breakfast table
a minute before the sun finds in me the password
that will let him be the first to unlock them from their helplessness
before he starts showing me how incapable I am to do it myself.

There, clutching the most fearful part of my character tightly in one hand
I thrust the other into my soul and grabbed
as much compassion as I could and clenched it in my palm.
I took it out, raised my hand as far above my head as I could,
unclenched my palm as gently as I could
and let all the compassion that my palm could fit in it
start untying one by one all the darknesses I carried with me.

I really wanted right then to see them
being swept away by the mild evening breeze
to somewhere where they can't spread terror anymore,
they can't hurt people anymore.
Thanks to you, tomorrow I won't roam my life's trails
trying to sell like a wandering street vendor
instead of tens of balloons tied with a string for kids,
tens of darknesses tied with mistakes for grownups.

Who said that all winters know how to end?
Two minds, one thought, half a mental nakedness.
Two bodies, one joy, half a dignity.

A winter ends when the most optimistic tree in the forest
gives birth to its first leaf.
That's why spring may be the laughter of nature.
Two full moons, one conscience, half a darkness.

Will you ever realize that this is the spot in my heart
where you were able to touch what I feel for you for the first time
when you chose to take from inside me
the wrong truth instead of the right lie?
I have the impression that this must be the laughter of a delusion
that no longer knows how to cry.
Eating from my logic's leftovers
I burped a future that contained a majestic emotional alibi.

So listen to what the words that will never be able to escape
the part of your mind
to which they never wanted to belong have to say to you.
Could this be the privilege of a lie that never knew how to ask its owner
if he wanted to liberate himself from of his truth?
It's my fault. I cut the darkness the night gave me in half
and took from inside it the part of my kindness
I had given my future to look after for me.

Dear God, who will protect me from my own knowledge?
Only if I stand on tiptoes can I see what I want to dream any longer.
Will you please let me talk to that "probably"
that's been waiting for me for hours at the edge of our fight
before I start arguing with the "maybe"
that I'm barely keeping from popping out of my mouth?

Those nights when going to sleep I end up after a few breaths
embracing the steepest peaks contained
by those midnights that are no longer satisfied with just bordering the night.
Please don't ask me to live a courage away from my fears!
To your health, great lover of the only free fall
you will never dare to throw in the pockets of your soul!

Don't worry, my silences know quite well how to reveal to you
anything I did not want to tell you.
Don't tell me that once again tonight
you didn't get a return ticket from the dreams
your self-awareness dreams on your behalf.
As soon as the light goes down,
the day's end sows questions all over your life
so that you'll stumble on the first answer
that will demand to have more daybreak than nightfall in it.

I would love to be able to unload all the stress
associated with my passage into tomorrow on the silences I use
to respond to the questions my past asks me.
Who would believe that there are treasures
that know how to survive in empty pockets!
When my life's trash demands to be its official translator.

The sunset today will refuse to believe
in all the dark colors the night forced it to bring along.
I spread as carefully as I can a fog around myself
so that the people I love won't be able to realize where I end
before I start figuring it out myself.
The moment in a person's life when the half-built truths
introduce themselves to the half-ruined consciences.

Joy of mine do you remember me? It's me.
Stop searching through my honesty's checkbook
for proof of how low I can fall.
Is this the sorrow felt by a man
who decided to spend the rest of his evening
dancing with the leftovers of his soul?

Well, this is what I learned cutting the reality you gave me as a gift
into so many little pieces
that my lies won't fit in them anymore.

all that hatred I gave birth to myself
but wasn't able to neutralize
by finding the courage to understand it.

I threw at its feet all the apologies
I found willing to swallow the strangled whisper
my silence makes out of all those sounds
it still hasn't learned yet how to hear.
It's the whisper that, every time I try to open my mouth
to persuade it to convey all that my soul just delivered to it,
forces me to compare the logical with the more logical
and any reality which can stand to live inside me
with my next failed confrontation with the most successful of my illusions.

In the maelstrom of the intensely primitive battle
I suddenly saw from afar the most beautiful blue window
I have even seen in my life.
It's the one whose only view is the dignity across,
the one I would have if I had become the person
I dreamt of being in my twenties.

I ran at once to climb through it
to try to save myself from the concessions
the last version of myself is ready to offer me.
I wanted so much to immediately surrender to those dreams
that don't mind listening to me talking for hours about what I fear,
but would never want me to help them find a way to decipher it.

Shutting this blue window as tight as I can
I want to lock up the most cowardly stains
my image is using to hide my true value from the people I love
in the part of my lungs where I've always stored those cries
that will never learn to write their happiness
on the echo they give birth to daily
and before noon they have already started demolishing.
The kiss of my life's next joy
just managed for the first time since my adolescence
to demystify the biggest darkness
which lives inside the smallest sunray that has ever shed its light on me.

a lesser conqueror, a lesser winner.

I sat in the twilight's comfortable embrace,
alone yet surrounded by all the guests my authenticity had invited,
listening to the pleas of my guilt,
which kept on asking me to do my best
to remove those of its own images from my past
it was never able to justify to me.

I covered my eyes with a truth
that insisted she wanted to be closer to a warm red than an apathetic brown,
a truth which the sunset let me take right out of its body,
and became the man who managed to love his trash
before convincing himself that he should start hating it.

sensing a few cloudy feelings of guilt away
the new secrets my life recently acquired
adjusting their dimensions
so I would still be able to pass in between them.

The invisible gratification that each new thing I buy rewards me with,
the one which my authenticity does everything she can not to notice,
began to awkwardly smile at me
because I hadn't yet begun to teach it how to cry.
I wonder, has the time come for me to stop hating
anything I cannot make my own?
How can I convince my greed to let me dream of things
that don't fit anywhere else
except for the smallest embrace
that my soul keeps at all times inside her?

Mistakenly mixing up the two silences of my life
that were born to hate each other,
I regrettably used the wrong one
to answer my greed's most important question of the day.

When I finished, I stumbled on one of those damn nights
which without warning came and stood
in the middle of the day right in front of me
demanding that my rage come immediately out to entertain them.
They are those nights that,
by opening their gates only for one person at a time,
force me to walk among the hungry leftovers
of the joy I wish I were able to feel
after every epic battle I fight with my own arrogance.

These are the moments in life when one feels
that by becoming the proud bodyguard of his most stainless stupidity
he begins to live closer to the extremities of his character rather than its core,
forcing his whisper to wrestle with his own scream
about which of the two will better represent him
in his coming battle with his next sorrow.

Once again I tried to wring
out of all the truth that I sense is trying to stay close to me
the one fairytale I will tell myself at night
to transform my indignation into tranquility,
hoping I'll finally manage to sleep.

So I began to create from scratch the brand new honesty I will use tomorrow,
out of all that my soul's defeats won't force me to remember today.
Hence I became the temporarily brilliant architect of my own malfunction
and at the same time the humble servant of my self-delusions.
This was one of the most emotionally illiterate moments of my life
when in a state of utter panic
I discovered that the person I know best in the world
is not myself.

I wrapped my truth as carefully as I could
around one of those favorite words of mine
I never understood what it wanted to confide to me before it began to speak,
and let it free to hang in the air around my mouth
until it falls on that silence of yours you consider most important of all.
Is this, I wonder, the right amount of ambiguity
my most impressive silence is hurriedly trying to hide inside me?
Be patient. You might be able to find out if you allow my lie to serve you properly.

Why, dear God, should the deliverance of a mind
that doesn't know how to acknowledge its own delusions
be the apology of an honesty
that would prefer to have been born
as one of its less important traits?
This is probably the reason that at the end of every sunset
man hesitantly opens the cash register of his soul
to find out how many redemptions it still has in it.
So many times at the end of a relationship I sat with my girlfriend
across from each other and opened with trembling hands
the cash register of our souls to find it completely empty!

Today is the day well-constructed hopes
would like to visit crumbling consciences.
Today is the day the minefield can't decide whom it wants to kill
and whom it wants to let live.
Who knows? Maybe today is the day I decide to stop being the eternal prisoner
of the oaths I swore to my self-confidence.

All that you saw when you finally went and sat down
on that shoreline at the edge of your heart
where my love put ashore those emotions of mine
that chose to be castaways
rather than disembark in a land they would never want to live in.
Tell me that now is the right moment to throw at your feet
all the hours I can no longer bear to be alone with my melancholy.
Is this what I felt when I sat for hours at the edge of my heart
unable to feel anything?

When every fight between us
has ended up being those moments of our life
when we both confront the side of our self we hate the most.
So the wonders that have been trapped in the mire of two hearts
which haven't found a way yet to feel sad the way they want
are about to give birth to a second chance.
Do you think these are the components of our common courage
which our next common decision doesn't know how to activate in me?

Teardrop. Indecisiveness. Strikingly beautiful envy.

I let the inadequacy of my brain explain to me
what every night that decides to end before midnight
has been trying for days to tell me.
Great anguish must be what a mirror feels
whenever it's called upon to provide an answer
that is designed to satisfy its owner's ego, not his truth.
Is that all that my pessimism helped you forget how to dream?

An illusion that knows how to do a good job
doesn't need to look in the mirror
to realize what it has done.
My arrogance no longer needs my next step
to tear me out of my compassion.
Perhaps today I will manage to figure out
what that point in our relationship
that starts living a minute before the gray in my life begins to curse me
has been shouting at me for some time now.

I think our relationship has reached a point
where one's emotional stains are asking permission
to clean anew the cleanest spot in the other's soul.
Do you think that this is the signature that the shadow of my melancholy left
on the part of your compassion that no longer wants to serve only you?
So that's how we managed to capture our gaze
in the sole darkness of our life
that our hopes recognize as equal to them.

When the fogs decided to stop working
for the ambiguity of their owners
and began to work for their ulterior motives.
Two adversaries who just before the battle refuse to translate for themselves
what victory has been insistently shouting at them for some time now.
My heart decided as of today
to no longer accept your emotional currency.

The moment in a man's life
when, inserting the key in a lock,
he is able for the first time to realize what freedom means.

more confident that I will be able to face
anything luck might try to trip me up with.

My success, having achieved quite a lot,
is now doing its best to learn how to be happy.
Can it? I doubt it…
All that I was taught through the years
never helped me understand
the massive wall made up of my own emotions
that is standing between me and my own success,
the one which has been threatening for some time now
to fall on me if I don't start paying more attention to it.

Every time I stand weak, almost unarmed
before my greatest enemy -my biggest fear,
I feel myself unwillingly kneeling,
retreating even from the smallest darkness
which found a way to hide in the most superfluous emotion of mine
that is standing two feet in front of me
and is staring me insistently in the eyes.

At that moment the creations of an amorphous inadequacy overwhelm my logic
and immobilize the optimism that I would like to believe permanently lives in my wings.
Facing this small but immensely powerful darkness
I stand frozen, with my feet stuck to the ground,
which doesn't stop sprouting new fears from its bowels every minute,
unable to convince any strength that belongs to me
to rush to get into my fist
before my indecisiveness finds its way there first.

The solutions evaporate right at the entrance door of my courage,
the waves of my own fear make a u-turn
and rush straight at me to drown me
and I, unable to figure out who my greatest enemy is right then,
the one I see, or the one I feel,
look for help, not from myself, but from others,
not just from other people but from other things.

Because what sweat doesn't resolve,
cheap, quick fixes are keen to jump in to help.
They are my chemical friends who are constantly waiting
behind the back side of each problem of mine
to re-introduce themselves to me and help me forget it,
transporting me as quickly and painlessly as possible
to a world which has no problems in it,
because it has no reality in it.

they can only be postponed for a few hours
after which they'll return stronger
while I'll return even weaker, more fearful
since, by seeking the help of my chemical friends,
I will have already lost another battle against them.

Struggling to honestly solve my problems on my own
I feel the drops of my sweat carrying them on their back
and as they come out of my skin they end up taking them away from me
to throw them into that self-serving divide
formed at the boundaries of my body with my cowardice
by the trash the poverty of my honesty has been freely dumping
on the next smile that is waiting at the edge of reality.

To win any fight outside my body
I must first win the one inside it.
When I learned how to fear,
I felt even stronger than when I learned how to hope.

in which the only thing that existed was an abandoned blue table
with a functionally indifferent steering wheel bolted to one side of it
and a comfortable driver's seat right next to it.

A few minutes later, the time remaining in your life
came and sat right next to you
and immediately began to make with its two hands small rusted square boxes
which, as soon as each one was finished, it politely offered to you.
These boxes contain the plots of land inside your head
which your sorrow and your joy
are forced to cultivate on your behalf every minute of your day.

It wasn't long before yesterday came
and sat prompt as always at the table.
It turned on its fascinating projector
and started showing you its highlights
as it saw them from its own point of view.
It's incredible how every day picks from its first hours
the weapon it will convince you to take in your hands
the next time it will force you to fight with your authenticity to the death.

As soon as the show was over
you felt the complete unwillingness of your brain to think
bleeding alternately on the table
one drop of self-confidence, one of stupidity and one of rust.
You already started seeing your next hour
coming to politely offer you on a red serving tray
painted with even more vivid red butterflies
the questions you will ask it one second before its own end,
when the last numbers on the clock
after almost a day of negotiation
will agree among themselves to show 59:59.

In those moments you couldn't find even a single thought of yours
willing to follow your logic to the end of your mouth.
You sat speechless, fascinated by the moment's incoherence,
surrounded by more kinds of silences that you ever thought existed-
silences which in the past under similar circumstances you would have already used,
freed from any mental obligation you might have
to seem worthy of what lives between your ears.

Realizing how reckless your self-control has become
you placed your sweaty hands on the steering wheel at the end of the table,
you gripped it tightly, but couldn't move it a single inch.
Unable to detach it from its uncompromising apathy
you saw yourself quickly turn from a driver
into a passenger of your own life.

unless you manage to first introduce it
to the part of your intellectual charm you call "Instinct".

Holding as tight as you can with both hands
the steering wheel of your personal sky,
you discover at the end of every minute that goes by
yet another color which your soul, no matter what happens, will never lend you
so you can start painting the coming day with it.

so that I'll become the castaway who besieged his own authenticity
before he was forced to rescue his salvation
from his own demystified lie.

I rush to plunge into the northern side of my life
where the light of the momentarily eternal smile
does not have enough time to detect my wounds
before I manage to hide them behind those words of mine
that have only very expensive dead ends in them,
the ones which keep on standing to my left and right
protecting me from any sorrow
I still haven't learned how to introduce to my joy.

In the sterilized sunset
the last sunbeams are departing without putting their signature
on the bottom right side of each dream of mine.
Their faint, almost unconscious light
that tries to illuminate my life without asking for my permission,
has already managed to sneak into the only heart around me
which has already dived into the summary of her own silence
to try to hide from my fury.

The emotional cheapness of the moment
immediately realized this and swiftly started using those colors,
which it had deliberately forgotten to bring with it,
to paint with the most fragile moves it had
the limits of my middle aged heart
on the part of my anger that still remains adolescent.
When it finishes, it promised me to visit my awkwardness
to explain what it did to any demystified optimism
that has the courage to still live inside me.

Surrounded by this faint light
and determined to experience for a while
the impunity of not being able to tell apart
what I feel from what I hope for,
I put my hand in my memory's left pocket
and took out a small mirror I had never seen before.
Staring at it I sensed the shape of my own despair
asking me to form, anyway it wants,
the cry contained in the first step
of the next hope my mind will give birth to.

The fake smiles dried quickly on the face
that does not believe in the emotions it is asked to express anymore,
a face that my lesser courage
had just managed to install on my head a few minutes ago.
True ingratitude was the only thing
I could find at the time waiting for me at the limits of my self-control
willing to follow me where I wanted to go.
The extravagant production of my heart's poverty
was now fading away on its own in front of the half open door
of the safe my life chose to lock my happiness in
to avoid having any contact with me.

I won't tell you what I feel.
I won't even tell you all that I can't feel.
I will throw myself between me
and my last glance in the mirror before I switch off the light
so it doesn't have time to reflect back to me
all that I begged it not to hide from me.

These are the retirement homes specializing in people
who never gave their age a chance
to explain to them how many new starting lines they can build together with it.

What I wouldn't give to be able
each time I am about to make an important decision in my life
to quickly figure out where my true knowledge ends
and where what I think I know begins!
I can't tell you how interested I am every time I speak with someone
in discovering as quickly as possible that part of his mind
where his knowledge ends and the intellectual fog begins,
the one he is doing his best to produce as fast as possible
so he won't realize, himself as well as the person he is talking to,
at which point of his arguments his truth demands to end before his lies begin.

My life really baffles me whenever it picks up speed
and hurls me head on at a decision of mine
that's waiting for me to make it while crossing as quickly as I can
the spot in my mind where my own knowledge is warning me
that it intends to withdraw in my next few words
before it starts embarrassing me.
Defeats don't come from what someone knows
but from what he chose never to learn.
It is the knowledge that upon reaching the end of his mind
helped him decide to take an easy step back
rather than a painful step forward.
It was the moment he chose the comfortable sofa,
which the most enchanting self-delusions of his
rushed to bring him so he can rest,
over climbing the steep uphill that true knowledge will gladly give as a gift
to everyone who decides to conquer it.

Oh, how enticing the temporary comfort that ignorance usually offers
to anyone who doesn't want to make an effort is!
What a truly horrible way to live!
After all, defeat is the revenge of all the things we never learned.

I don't know I have.
Sensing that, my next step suddenly forgets its operating instructions
and starts walking alone towards my future.

Talking for hours with everything I am afraid of
my soul starts painting, using the most languid, deep blue moves she has,
her own absence around the most hesitant borders of my life.
The all-white fear which my own ashes at that point beget
anxiously runs to hide my second face from me,
the one it's certain I fear
since I've never seen it before.

What other fears do my fears hide inside them?
The fastest way to reach the redeeming light
contained in the answer to this question
is to pass directly through the heart of the first darkness I come upon
while running as fast as I can towards my sorrow.
You see, the darkness that wants to have more white in it
than what the pessimism of the people around it allows it to have,
no matter how hard it tries, cannot be copied onto a human soul.
And I, no matter how hard I try, cannot convince my logic to repackage her victories
in such a way that, avoiding to interpret her greatest weaknesses,
she ends up introducing herself only to those character flaws of mine
that prefer to live in the optimistic part of my mind.

It's incredible how victory invents in my head
the trophies she would like to win
faster than defeat manufactures the silences
which she will soon be forcing one after the other
to come and try to comfort me.
Fear is not yet sure from which point of my future
it should begin destroying the white in me it so admires.

Doing everything I could to survive
I threw all the fears I could round up
into that amorphous corral in my head with the colorful barbed wire around it,
hoping I'll be able to make them fear the energy of the optimism
which that beautiful spring day that permanently lives inside me always felt.

Each fear I locked up managed, as I was tossing it in,
to slap another set of handcuffs on me.
The more of them I forced inside, the weaker I ended up feeling.
Looking me in the eyes they passed before me one by one
leaving their fingerprints on the surface of those cries
coming from the image of a man
who was just then starting to realize
what was never supposed to happen to him.

waiting for me to decide if I believe more in my insecurities
that they do in me.
Today I feel that my optimism will teach me again
how to wash off the colors my self-confidence uses
to paint my time onto the last red dusk
that it is willing to leave behind with me to nurse
until I hand it back to it tomorrow afternoon.

I took a deep breath
before I began to breathe the way optimism wanted,
I questioned what I forgot to believe in,
threw myself into the most inexpressible cry of my self-criticism,
convinced my palms to toss their own melody
into the lesser questions of my misgivings,
and started painting my night
with the whitest white I could find laying around me
that was waiting for me to start attacking myself without anybody's help.

I really hope that the road my soul will be using tonight
to reach the starting point of my next happiness
will remember how to lead me to the heart
where my true dimensions live.

that's been waiting for days now just outside my next happiness
to meet with me.

I don't know how to make the exhausted trust that you still have in me
consent to touch the sharpest edges of my words
to verify that they're not as annoying as they seem.
I sense its light inside me hesitate,
as if afraid to embrace the boundaries of my beliefs,
lest it ends up crushing them.

The first thing a mirror learns
is to hide beneath its surface for future use
pieces of the self-confidence of the person
who needs to use it on a daily basis.
Same thing with mine.
Using all the tricks it has learned
from those fleeting glances I've aimed at it,
while pretending that I was not looking,
it is determined to rewrite the operating instructions
of the conscience that I should use from now on
the way it perceives them.

Every sunset I feel the enemy of my bravery
slowly dying in the suspended palm
my heart uses to measure the immensity of my insignificance.
I feel like I don't fit in my words anymore,
my mistakes don't fit in their own shadow any longer.

Trying to free myself from anything that lives illicitly in me
I started running with as much courage
as the courage running next to me had
toward the solitary but greedy whisper I could not avoid hearing.
It's the whisper I hear coming from the spot
where each morning my megalomania meets
with all those questions it's been meaning to ask me for some time now.
Oh, how much I want to prove to myself
that I am still capable of stealing my self-reliance
from my most heavily built misgivings!

Amazingly, somewhere between the pain of truth
and the vain enjoyment of lying,
lives a soul whose aim in life is to get to know again
one by one those darknesses of hers
which long ago shaped the path she is following today.

which was made of square cubes of light blue water.
To the left of the wall's center a disproportionately small door had sprung up.
It is right at this entrance that the stroll through my delusions decided to end.
You see, every man who doesn't find the courage to defend his truth
finds a way to construct his own end out of his biggest lie.

On the inexplicably beautiful yellow and black crossword puzzle
painted on every square inch of the front door
I recognized something which, though I had never seen it before in my life,
I was immediately sure that I belonged to it.
I think it was the entrance of my own truth.

I didn't dare ring her doorbell,
lest I automatically become the undignified lover of my hesitations.
I stood for hours like a fool letting the doubts I had right then
come out of my body and voluntarily undress
in front of those vividly red happy whispers
coming from those parts of my soul which my malice hates,
the ones I could barely hear anymore
every time they decided to talk to me.

Looking for ways to solve the huge illuminated crossword puzzle
which the very door had devised
in the corner of the time of my life that I had left mentally unused
I felt thousands of colorful words
that contained at least one yellow and black letter
crowding between the ground I was standing on
and those mistakes of mine
which I wanted at that moment to throw as far as I could
hoping they'll find a shred of a bigger lie
where they could survive without the slightest help from me.
These are the moments of one's life when he feels
that no matter how fast his mind races
he cannot escape the attacks
of the most predatory part of his stupidity.

Breathing with difficulty,
crammed among those leftovers of my knowledge
that always despised me,
I tried, as quickly as I could, to self-direct my stupidity
hoping I could make it seem less repulsive.
No matter how hard I tried, I couldn't.
I wrestled with myself for hours in front of that door,
which, as time went by, started smiling mockingly at me,
taking on a harsh, almost vengeful nuance.

Mentally defeated I turned, as I always do every time I see my logic
throw the white towel into the ring of my next sorrow,
to the questions that my compassion had to ask me.
I stayed alone with my soul for hours
listening to what my mind was trying to whisper to me
using a sound I had never heard before.
As midnight drew nearer,
it insistently kept on proposing
golden but bankrupt solutions one after the other
while, having already turned its back on me,
it was quickly moving away trying to get into my next day before I did.

The night is ready to steal the cry it had given me earlier
from within the latest despair that I feel.
All I ask of my biggest fear in these moments
is to find the courage in it to propose marriage to the free fall
which I unintentionally started building right in front of me
using only the fingers of my hands
that have long lost the ability to count.

It seems I overfilled the lies of my life
with the kind of truth that never realized
how many draws I asked it to hide on my behalf inside it.
The moment when what I am able to see
will synchronize again with what I am able to feel,
my soul will decide to welcome me back into her truth.
The first word in the crossword puzzle just found its answer.
My soul evidently knows how to hide her own peacefulness
in various places inside my future that only she can find.

The delusions we came up with during those moments of that fight
which was born long before we two met
demand once again to make us their accomplices.
Maybe this way I will manage to become a truth that just tossed the script
reality had written for it into the trash.

When your pain decided to take my truth in hand
to write slogans on the giant stone walls
midnight just finished building in the middle of my heart
so I can't see today who I'll become tomorrow.
Do you think that's the reason the noise made by the eraser
tomorrow holds in its hand when it passes over the questions today has
sounds so soothing?
There are no sudden silences,
only souls that just stopped trusting their own words.

A man dies happy if he manages even once in his life
to meet with the reason he lived.
When words stop writing,
silences start erasing.
Why should these be the hours when realities
get into fights with our greatest truths just to annihilate them?

The moves a toxic look uses to erase kindness
from a discussion that does not want to end
before truth finds a way to dry the blood
on the fists of the words that seek to hurt
before they understand what they are trying to say.
What wouldn't a coma give to be able to learn
how to do the job of a full stop!
This is probably the deposit truth makes at the end of every sorrow
in the account of the beautiful side of reality.

Letting my eyes wear the look
a nakedness uses when staring at anybody around it that's not naked.
Maybe this is the conspiracy organized by an instant catharsis
against chronic delusion.
Don't ever let your wear and tear rewrite on your gaze
the part of your capabilities that it never understood.

All that a starting line will never confide to you
after you start running.
When a person's beliefs have stopped caring
about making his life happier.
Do you realize that with every backward step you take
you surrender yet again to that point in your life
where only those versions of yourself
that strive to be uglier than you survive?

Only when you finish, will you find inside you the point you started from.
Will you please give me tonight one of those darknesses of yours
that haven't decided yet what color they want to be
so I can dress it up as a dawn?
It's the time when truths rush into their owner's mind
and start ripping out those thoughts of his
that bloom only in its most fertile spots.

Maybe that's why my melancholies write better poems than me.

Perhaps the blue sky every morning ultimately begins
with every promise one makes to himself as soon as he wakes up
that today he will try to make every moment of his life
happier, not easier.
Do you think that's why every time I discover
that no matter how hard she tries, my soul cannot fly any higher
I realize how low my logic has already fallen?

You see, no one knows a man as well as his own happiness.
She knows by heart all the tricks he employs to deceive her,
to make her his by any horrible, dishonest means
and so she ends up calmly sitting a few feet away
each time using a new, unorthodox way
to let him believe that by simply defeating his misery
he will manage to make her his own.

Fortunately there are people around me who love me enough
to rescue me from the battle with my happiness!
Hearing your soul's laughter coming from afar,
most likely not from the farthest point but from the darkest,
my heart urges me to take a step forward
so I can fall on the next minute of my life
that is more enthusiastic than me,
the next minute which even before it's born
has declared to me that it won't let me touch it with my dirty hands
so I can try to make it feel more ordinary, more sad.

How stingy can a heart be
that has no more space for emotions
because her owner has filled it with thousands of multiplications and divisions?
I'm certain that the moment I figure it out
I'll discover how much generosity
my biggest fear can hold in it.
It's been proving it to me for years now after all!

Hearing me approach,
my steps try not to hear those words of mine shouted at them from afar
by the parts of my future which my adolescence never wanted me to visit
without my enthusiasm being present,
and start walking towards the part of my mind
from which for months now
not even a single new thought has dared to emerge.

how I managed to lift out of bed a body similar to mine
which, however, had another heart in it, a much smaller heart
than the one I went to sleep with the night before.

It really annoys me when, having no way to be more human
without appearing to be less of a winner,
I end up letting the coldness of the people around me
flirt with any part of my compassion
I left deliberately unguarded!
I'd really love to let my enthusiasm
convince me to get drunk by slowly sipping
every second of my life that wants to be cheerful
before I'm forced to become the man who escaped from his happiness
because he couldn't stand living away from his sorrow.

Is there anyone, I wonder, who doesn't know
why he wants to live as far away as possible from his own laughter?
Maybe one who's afraid that by managing to do that
he will end up running into the reasons why
the perfection he's been pursuing all his life
has announced to him that it's better to be perfect and miserable
than mediocre and happy.

Hearing this dilemma grab every word I utter
and lay it as carefully as it can
on the most sensitive part of your truth,
I wonder if I will ever manage this way
to rob our relationship of its unhappiness,
to steal myself from my hypocrisy,
to pilfer the golden death of an innocence
from inside the ugliest dream
the luck that has long hidden in my life's next decision
can dream on my behalf.

for as long as a few minutes of unidentifiable sorrow may last,
between my own illusions
and the ones that my self-control does not need anymore
to function properly.

It comes, well-intentioned as always,
to help me escape through those thoughts of mine
for which I still haven't learned how to dig to lay their foundations
in the part of my mind whose ground is completely safe
from the tremors which sooner or later my cowardice will cause.

The moment my silence heard them coming
it disappeared as quickly as it could from my face
and hid in the back side of my lips,
where my words spend their time training their own image
before going out to impress anybody
I cannot win over by simply displaying my truth.

Without knowing why, I set out to deform my own fingers
to the point where I started feeling their own thoughts
moving through my body trying to discover
which of its parts is the one responsible for my stupidity
and which one for the dreams my silence dreams on my behalf.

My mind's main street realized for the first time
that the time has come to change its address.
It knows that wherever it goes, my soul will find it
because she really insists on teaching its imperfections how to become happier,
its deepest, most carnivorous crevices how to not need more pieces of my soul
to plummet in them so they can feel full.

The delivery man of those triumphs of my sorrow
that after all these years are still disappointed by me
finally came to bring me what's left of a drop of sweat
which didn't get a chance to die
because it decided to try.
Marveling at this drop's courage
my soul stayed up all night till the morning sun granted her the right
to fall asleep lying on the first sunbeam it sent down to meet her.

In the haze that a second opinion keeps on lavishly bestowing on me
I finally met the strength of the first one.
I took courage from my own scream
and asked my next sorrow to come clothe me whenever she wants
with those fabrics of hers that are made of cynical velvet thorns.

where the one's vanity fought last night
with the dreams the other's flaws were dreaming at the time.

It's those stainless-steel dreams
that each daybreak finds lying on
the only completely corroded teardrop
which for years has been trading my enthusiasm
with anyone interested in exchanging it for his own boredom.

There, confronted by the sorry image of this transaction,
I discovered that I don't detest any spot on my body more
than the one that gives birth to my apathy.
It's the spot that, as hard as I've tried,
I was never able to justify its existence to my happiness.

To this teardrop I have nothing to confess.
I have nothing to hide from it either.
I have nothing else though to offer the sunset
except for all that the night will need
in order to answer the questions
this teardrop intends to ask it soon.

My conscience is ready to throw its youngest questions
into the fire of my soul.
I lay on the bed, ready to become the lover of the time I've got left
before I become the leftovers of the time I have left.
Nothing lasts forever
except all that never dared to be born.

after many tries was able to convince me
to become the disingenuous ambassador
of the part of my life that remains unexplained.
It wants me to become the representative of the illiterate residue of truth
to which my most valuable malfunctions bestow my shape,
a travelling defender of the absence of the ideas
in which I always passionately believed.

My next step was already slowly fading away,
losing all its enthusiasm to move forward,
when it finally decided after many hours
to stand up to everything my emotional poverty
has been whispering in my ears for some time now.
It's those undignified sounds
that discovered me for the first time
when they saw me dueling with my insomnia.

Together with my cowardice they kept on constantly watching me for days
attempting once in a while to lock me up even for a few minutes
in the drawer where the carnivorous guilt of the minimal fear lives,
the fear that never stops hovering around me
trying to sell me the new dimensions of my own cowardice.

For some time now I've stopped trembling
every time I hear the heavy footsteps of my conscience coming,
not only from the edge of my heart that prefers to live next to my present,
but even from further away to berate me.
Without aiming to, during a lesser summer I became
the lucrative loan shark of my most insatiable breakdowns.

Learning how to better protect the palm of my hand
from what my caress wants to force it to forget how to do,
I became the highly paid caretaker of all those mistakes of mine
that demand to devour my virtues
before I have time to realize that they are no longer exclusively mine.

I hung any questions my conscience has
behind the lightly rusted entrance of my mouth
and started talking using colorless silences
instead of flashy words.
Do you think that "silence" may be what we call these moments in our lives
when we decide to bury our most precious dreams
in the remotest part of our soul
so we can't easily touch them?

Do you think that's how a soul's audition
for the biggest part in her life actually starts?
Uncaring, you shouted at me: "Tell me, how's the view
from the lowest point of your greatest sorrow?"
Does pride include an end?
Does truth include a silence?
It does, if the full stop at the end of the last sentence spoken
still feels proud of the person who used it.
Does self-criticism have any more asterisks in it to present to an ego
that keeps acting as if it doesn't realize the damage it is causing?
Let me ask my arrogance.
Do you think today I will finally come up with an answer
that fits the dimensions of my self-confidence?

For some time now I've been hearing the sounds
hidden inside the colors my life sees every time I look the other way
lean over and whisper in my ear
that they can't stand belonging to me any longer.
You see, only through the part of my imagination that has long been living in them
can they communicate with me anymore.
Do you think I've become the man who has the ability to see the dreams
that the people he loves can't see?

I am almost ready to let one of the most ruthless apologies I ever had
fight alone with all the means at its disposal
to mend the damage I have been inflicting almost daily since we first met
on the end of our relationship.
I think it's time I asked my pride
to hide me inside it for a while
so that any strength of mine that today decided it wants to hurt me
won't be able to find me.

For forty years now every morning the dawn sits down with me
to teach me how to rebuild my beginning,
how to fashion the good-morning I will later wish
in such a way that I'll convince it
to love all the optimism I will pour in it
more than the gray cloud I see every time I look inside me.
Every morning I try to rebuild my beginning
from all those thousands of moments in my life
when I turned my back on joy itself
preferring to warmly embrace any other emotion
I could feel at the time.

That moment I decided to sit for the first time
next to the personal moments in my life
during which I was afraid of myself
more than I feared anyone else,
the moments during which I was so frightened
that I briefly believed I had reached the point of betraying who I am
to become someone who, if he could stand opposite his own beliefs,
after a while would see them throw up in disgust.

that doesn't let him become who he wants to be?

Years ago, on one of those Sunday mornings when I set out
not knowing what I have to do to keep winning throughout the day that's coming
without compromising any of my principles,
while I was staring at the early morning
as it was trying to trip up my only just awaking mind,
a sunbeam charged my eyes and whispered to me:
"Ask your sorrow where she wants to take you today
and start running as fast as you can in the opposite direction".

Avoiding to believe all those emotions that are trying to make me feel
more confusingly successful that naively serene,
I began to walk on that beautiful lit by golden lights fashion runway
vanity had set up in the center of my head.
The longer I kept walking,
the more I saw the parts of my character I respect the most refuse to follow me.
They stayed many feet behind me
on the first square inch of runway where, no matter how hard I shouted,
they had convinced themselves they couldn't hear me.

So I set out to cross the beginning of my sorrow
until I reached the end of the happiest Fall I have ever experienced
which hours ago had come and parked itself in the middle of my life.
I walked to the end of the dirt road time had brought
and set down before my most courageous step.
I walked to the end of that runway,
or was it the end of my self-confidence -I can't remember
and tried to turn my body to go back,
but was unable to.
I felt as if an invisible wall
had been following for hours a few steps behind me.
It had come and, without me realizing,
had raised its body right behind my back,
pushing me gently but insistently.

Terrified I looked in front of me
and the farthest I tried to look,
the more I couldn't see what was happening a few inches away from me.

than what she thought.
The last thing left for me to do
was to muster all the reserves of charm remaining
in the flattery my mind uses
to make me seem more handsome than stupid,
and not more ugly than smart.

I tried to steal my heart from inside the ashtray
in which she extinguishes her cigarette butts,
I tried to steal the rainbow from that patch of sky
where it assured me itself its end was to be found,
I tried to steal myself from that part of my soul
where she assured me the end of my sorrow permanently lived,
but I wasn't able to.

My biggest shortcoming is that my happiness
believes in my perfectionism.
For the first time I felt that I no longer need any of my footsteps
except for those that only want to take me backwards.
Having nowhere else to go
I hurriedly plunged into that void at the end of the hallway,
the void made for me by all those emotions of mine
which believe that they have no reason to live in me any longer.
You see, the steepest cliffs
are not formed by nature where mountains end
but by one's human nature at the spot where his soul no longer wants to exist.
Taking a decisive step forward
I lost yet another faceless hell that lived all these years inside me,
perhaps the last one.

the one I was told since childhood
that I should never attempt to define, start.

While searching, I stumbled on my age.
The various impasses it always cultivated in me
have always been content to live amid the most colorful stains
painted by those precious teenage emotions of mine
which, as hard as I've tried all these years,
I still haven't managed to feel.

I am getting older and more than ever I need
to at least try to gently touch even the least important emotion
my soul is able to give birth to.
I want to leave no feeling inside me unborn,
nor deny any flavor of my soul
from doing its best to sweep me off my feet.
This inability of mine to achieve that
likes so much to be reflected by the anxiety I feel every time I'm left alone
watching the next day's yet unborn guilt
rush in after a few minutes to entertain me.

So I reach the end of a darkness made out of steel,
inhaling with difficulty in my every breath
the precious ruins left behind by the innocence I never realized I had,
hearing their echoes trying to tear my eardrums to shreds.
The sly devils are struggling on their own
to build me from scratch a more battle-ready toughness
which can work together with the panoramic weakness it sees inside me
better than I do.

Lying on my back, with my body immobilized
between the cynical truth of the moment
and the superfluous lie of the next one,
I see the sunset, using its most mincing mannerisms,
yielding with every passing minute its colors to my melancholy
which, having embraced them one by one,
eagerly thrusts them as deep as it can
into the memory that my happiness has exclusively reserved
for all those things it doesn't have to remember.

I hope this way I'll be able to finally read
that which, by lowering my chin and turning my gaze
towards the most unsatisfied spot within me
I never managed to see.

The noose made by a conscience
which does everything not to betray her owner
whirls around the neck of a soul which has lost consciousness
and is trapped in the quicksand of the great ambiguity
awaiting someone to rescue her.

Frozen in the gravity of the questions
my logic keeps on bringing up in front of my self-control
I spot on the countless little sand dunes
which have formed at the end of my imagination
thousands of tiny castaways,
each having a thought of mine in their embrace,
running from the shore back to the sea
to save themselves from the voracious appetite
of the brand new fears I gave birth to a short while ago.
Dusk always had the ability to uncover inside me,
a heart which I never managed to locate.
I kissed on the mouth the agony my logic felt at the time
while I tenderly looked in the eyes
the reasons my happiness wanted to acquire a second heart
because the one I have can't bear to operate properly anymore.

The night began to enfold me in its most precious questions
and I, obliged to hang out with my emotional boredom's ambition,
started blowing up one by one
all the bridges that lead to what I always wanted to feel
to prevent me from crossing over to it
before I am able to understand it.

my sorrow called me from afar to talk to me
before I had time to switch sidewalk to avoid her.

Forced to immediately start washing off my fresh questions
in the silence that my cynicism so eagerly keeps on lending me,
I begin to feel things I don't understand,
smile at what I fear the most,
borrow any "yes" from those misgivings of mine
that do everything they can to keep it for themselves,
and any "no" from the certainty of knowing that I have no other option
but to believe so little in my own beliefs.

I only have an hour left to convince my day to not be afraid,
to not regret what she eventually had to become,
to not insist on wanting to sell to my serenity
all that she is not willing to buy from her.
I won't let the recently decommissioned century of my golden sorrow,
which lurks behind my most glorious guilt,
grab me by the legs and throw me
into the thick mud where my most disappointed unspoken words live.

Dreams today won't die before they are forgotten.
I promise myself that by the end
of the deepest breath my body can draw in
I will have managed to climb out of the most faceless laughter of mine
to finally see if I've learned how to breathe
in a way that my optimism approves.

I nailed the first sunbeam that landed in front of my feet
on the least optimistic crevice I found
wedged in my soul's only steep rock face
which seemed less vertical than me,
placed on my back the only two smiles I could find in me
which at the time were refusing to smile,
and started to climb.

The time has come for me to rebuild my laughter from scratch
and fill it with as much tomorrow as I can find searching through yesterday.
I want to have a laughter
that will turn to me, look me in the eyes and demand from me
by the end of the day to have succeeded
in turning the very huge nails that live inside me toward the kind sunset,
hoping that it will be able to convert them into pins.
It's evidently true.
Love is the art of the unspoken word.

leap out of the emptiness in every darkness
that does not know why the color of what it is made of is only black.
They come to wrap my body around your sadness
to remind me that I need their awful caress
more than the splendor of the first morning sunbeam
I will not be able to see tomorrow
unless I manage to unlock it from the infinity I feel
every time I can't understand where my own minimal ends.

It's this very emptiness that I constructed myself
a few months after the end of my adolescence,
in the months between the time I invented my own scream
and the reconciliation with the forced landing
of a youthful heart that never learned how to hurt others without hurting herself.
Ah, those forced landings on the surface of the kind of dreams
that my enthusiasm let me dream at the time even in the middle of the day...
When a person is left alone with his soul
and to feel safe needs to switch on a light,
then he knows that from that moment on
he belongs to his most indignant darkness.

I tried with every odd move I discovered
in the most abandoned warehouses of my body
to empty as much shadow as I could from inside me
on any joy I found around me
and at the same time to find a way to convince the sun
to shine more rays on me for the rest of the day
so I can see deeper between the crevices of my heart
hoping I'll manage to discover what my emotional stinginess
allows me to believe in from now on.

Shining the enormous yet extremely frightened floodlights of my logic
on my more mentally developed delusions,
I saw the figures of some impatient old words of mine
running like crazy up and down my brain
trying to find a way to escape
from what my desperation wants to make me try to achieve next.
Leaping over my mind's highest walls
they run to get away from it
before it manages to arrest them and lock them up forever
in its most unanswered questions.

Suddenly a delusion, which until recently
hadn't realized that it was mine,
escaped the attention of my self-preservation
and began to run in the opposite direction than all the others,
trying to wedge itself as deep as it could
in what it considered to be the safest place in my mind.

It came to fight, to win back from me the absurdity of my truth,
to help me get away from everything that happens in my life
about which I can't decide whether I should start feeling it
or stop trying to make it part of my logic.

I put one foot of the first thought that came to my mind
in front of the other, which continued to hesitate,
loaded any words which at the time were dozing at the edge of my lips
on the scrawny lie I just began to paint on my freshest phrase,
and began to rinse my body
of any fog that found the courage to hug me today.
By the way, you still haven't told me,
how many silences do you think are hidden in what I just told you?

I could utter right then.
Looking at me straight in the eyes,
and without feeling the slightest fear,
it said to me slightly upset:
"You have one minute to choose between your soul, her darkness and me".

My logic really fears those five impeccably dressed words
which refuse to negotiate with the greenest hue
that the soil that lives inside me has.
And I, running breathless
among all that I still think I know how to fear
but not how to be afraid of,
try to get away from the overambitious mouthfuls of guilt
that my cowardice hasn't stopped for a while feeding me with.
Those obnoxious devils for the first time in my life
decided just a few minutes ago to jointly hound me
to exterminate, not me, but my smile.

I just installed new spare parts on my courage
and sent it out into my reality
so it can manage to strip my defeatism of its strength,
perhaps even its will to win,
bringing back to me all the sentimental currency I spent
to learn how to pay back the debt
I owe to those who I manage to lose from.

I can no longer keep on cultivating inside me
those four minutes I bought from my greediest misgivings.
Disregarding me, they continue to maintain in parallel with mine
a separate, private, inhospitable past,
a past which unfortunately turned out to be much more capable
at explaining my life to my future
than to me.

The skillful burglar of all the black
I pretend, while it clearly no longer belongs to me,
that I still safeguard in the most bankrupt safe inside me,
asks to stay forever in the place he just broke into,
but not in the treasure he just acquired.

that for the last few hours I've been giving birth to on my own.
I keep on hitting it in the face
to try to persuade it to confess to me
how many favors it has already promised my past
to let me enter my future whenever I want.

My solitude decided today to dawn just for me
a few minutes before midnight
and a few sorrows after I met my latest version,
the one I will present to the people I love
a few minutes after I conclude my negotiations
with the flipside of my beliefs.

Looking at one of them in the eyes
I realized how much I was missed by the person I never managed to become.
No matter how hard she looks,
my life does not have with her any more coupons of future joy,
just happiness that demands to be immediately cashed in, right this minute.

While the one question eternity wants to ask me
is not yet ready to become the most heavily armed tear of the moment,
my serenity keeps asking me
to let it last as long as my kindness does.
How strange! Those moments of my life
that never intended to waste their time
dealing exclusively with me
came one by one to my bedside
and asked to reintroduce themselves to me.

There won't be a next sunshine
unless the sky finds a good reason to not tear from inside it
the kind of blue that will want to lend its color to gray
so that the next cloud can be born.
There won't be a next joy
unless I find a reason inside me not to give birth to an emotion
that will refuse to be anything else than my next sorrow.
How sure am I that I like the fact
that I have built a world around me, within me that believes that?
In order to confidently answer that
I should probably convince my lungs
to release those fugitive from my logic words of old
that knew how to heal before they began to hurt.

But why am I telling you all this?
Past glories, past glories…
All this I handed over to be looked after
by the first step my vanity managed to climb
before I even decided if I wanted to climb it myself.
Now, unable to fit all the rage that I feel
into any blackness in my life
that's already more pessimistic that it can stand to be,

considers it her obligation to carry a sledgehammer with her wherever she goes
so she can smash into a thousand pieces anything she cannot create herself.

Truth just decided to get up from next to me
and slam the door behind her.
I am left alone, faced with the phony sunshines
that one after another peel off the freshly renovated faces
of the morally bankrupt personalities
I see on the TV in front of me
flooding with their heavily armed lies its entire surface.
These are the personalities that don't care whether
by stuffing some more currency of cheap splendor in their pockets
they end up making the world around them
more charmingly inhumane, more brilliantly blurred.

I am so disappointed by all the possessions
my disappointment has offered me so far!
I see the different kinds of abyss
that, as soon as I turn on the TV, start living on its surface
insistently asking me to let them speak right away
to the abyss that lives inside me.
They want so much to persuade it to start building bigger warehouses at once
so it can fit inside them the larger clouds
they will soon help me start giving myself as gifts.

the supernatural entertainer of her worst fears.

It should be no surprise then
that seeing you sitting right across from me,
almost a whole sadness away from me,
I simultaneously feel that your biggest defeats are already living inside me.

I cry because you begin to cry.
I cry because you begin to cry
the moment you touch my very expensive inner wasteland,
wondering how I manage so successfully
as soon as I wake up every morning
to immediately put to sleep those invisible emotions of mine
I was never able to figure out if I feel them more than they feel me,
how I manage to live a mile away
from those pickpocket paradises that live inside me,
how I manage to simultaneously live inside the trash I want to throw out
and away from everything in my life
I just have not found a way yet to keep close to me.

Using all twelve cameras that are at my intelligence's disposal
I'm trying to find a way to figure out what I feel.
I cannot.
I cannot see because I have already sold my very last radiance
to the success I am trying to convince my humility that I deserve.
I sold the very last rainbow I had
to the safe where my luck keeps all the monochrome tomorrows she owns.
I sold the interpretation of my life to every one of her moments
I chose to be mean and successful
rather than kind and average.
It's in these moments when a man discovers that his next day
belongs more to his past than to him.

Would you please be kind enough to lend me
two echoes of your laughter
so I can learn again how to touch all that I cannot grasp,
two smiles so I can learn again how to love those parts of my character
my ego never allowed me to even get close to?
Only your love knows
how to uproot from inside me that almighty shapeless desert,
a sweet remembrance at a time,
from the private past that has been installed in my brain
by every silence which ever lived inside me that never dared to speak to me.

I really want, even for just a few moments,
to wrap my hands around my most toxic thoughts
before I let them free to go out and start destroying
everything I struggled so much to learn anew
how to shelter in the most anxious part of my fist.
Only to you can I entrust anymore
all those emotions that I am afraid to let my heart feel.
Love. Winter. The optimistic balance of an adolescence. Springtime desolation.

took from our hands the steering wheel of our lives
and led us to the clearing
at the edge of which the dark becomes darker before it becomes affable,
shadows become impenetrable walls before they become warm embraces.
It's the clearing that the rules of our lives have concocted
to hide themselves from our happiness,
the one where they feed their wounds every morning
so they will have the strength till the end of their shift late at night
to go on hurting any person they find before them.

Today I feel that, somewhere between dawn
and the first draw of the day,
we will find the courage to take a step sideways
and, embracing the secrets that our smallest private miracle
has been keeping from us for some time,
we will be able to touch those beautifully toxic questions
our relationship's least recognizable cowardice
always wanted to ask us.

These are the questions whose echoes
profusely bleed heretic threats,
those questions that always feared
that we would agree to answer them
only if that insolent emotion of ours
that makes us less cowardly than our greatest cowardice
were to ask them.

The eyes of our souls breathed a sigh,
and so did the predatory stowaways of our truth.
The pain became milder, more transparent, more understandable.
Most of the shadows that are still in love
with the emotions they belong to
took a long and self-serving step back,
every deep crevice of our logic
that is still in love with the faceless advent of suffering
bowed its head for yet one more time,
our passion found the strength once more
to go out into the streets of our soul to demand a better future.
Our hearts began again to crave one less lock,
maybe even a few more echoes of the sun's enthusiasm,
the ones he let us have only when we are temporarily out of excuses
to accuse him for all the good that he is doing us.

before it gives a chance to any other color to introduce itself to her.
Every moment of our life
will again demand to have one less melancholy
than the ones our most ambitious flaws
are fighting tooth and nail to squeeze in it.

A fight. Midnight. Almost true.
How much more arrogance can fit in
the midpoint of the word "divorce"?
We will find out when the triumph of black and white logic
becomes the defeat of a colorful truth.
Perhaps also when the varnish of a lie refuses to be so shiny.

1 couple that fights
consists of two players of the same team who, to satisfy their insecurities,
decide to become rivals for a while,
that is until the moment their insecurities are secured again.
Hence they end up becoming effigies
of their own hollow promises they make to their beliefs
which will start falling in love with their shortcomings one after another
when they realize that the moment has come
when their kindness, unable to live with them,
will quickly run to hide in the back part of the first fake reality that will let it in.

We both burrow as fast as we can
to dig out an emotional canyon
so that we can hide from any negative emotion within us
that keeps on doing all it can to force us to admit
that you can triumph even by losing.
Taking out of the pockets of each of our souls
the shadows of those emotions that keep us captive in our malice
and leaving them on the table,
we start asking for the return of those shortcomings of ours
which during previous fights,
having first carefully wrapped them in our most able words,
without thinking much, we hurled at each other's face.

When we were done, we were impressed
by how many more than we thought they actually were.
We both felt really strange
when staring at us critically, they began to explain to each one of us
how much shorter we are than our actual height.
It's not coincidental that forcing our soul to wear heels
helps us feel better about lying to our truth.

How much longer will we have to carry with us wherever we go
the most ambitious secrets our sorrow does all it can to prevent us from finding out?
While one's future has already started
negotiating with the other's insecurities
for all that he hopes to be able to understand
by asking his biggest questions what they think of him,
each one of us in a different way
has already started cheating on his kindness
with those feelings of guilt of his he found inside it.

of every delusion we created together all these years.
We wanted so much to hide inside them
hoping we'll manage to escape the attacks of our less visible beliefs,
but the only thing we were able to accomplish after many hours
was to fit in our two souls one and a half self-confidence and half a truth.
Ah, those plunders of conviction,
the looting of a self-confidence that grew tired
of believing so much in itself…

The minimal chaos we both rushed to hide in today's midnight,
which wants to ask our permission
to not be as black today as we forced it to be,
hesitantly approached the last life jacket
our reality has at its disposal.
It just wants so much to puncture it!
It wants to puncture it so that it won't give us another chance
to escape the attacks of our self-criticism.
It's so strange to hear the chaos which you created yourself,
using the strongest convictions you have in you,
request from the ending the first day of a relationship has forever kept inside it
to ask each of our shortcomings separately
what we owe it for its services.

Each minute we spend wounding each other with our words
gets even angrier when it sees that the deeper we get into our fight
the more our skin draws back from our fingers,
which just a few hours ago were tenderly touching each other's melancholy,
revealing the aggressive claws that spring up from the storm
which we ourselves give birth to within us during those moments.

It's this handmade storm
which for some time has stopped respecting us
and has started booing us loudly.
No matter how much sorrow or blackness that storm drinks from inside us
it can no longer quench its thirst.
It wants to destroy, not only everything we have built,
but everything we have felt.
It wants to hunt down any beautiful emotion we have shared
until it finds it and stomps on it, destroying it
and making it regret it was so beautiful.
I was always left with my mouth hanging open each time I realized
what a great renewable source of energy my meanness is,
especially the one that demands to totally destroy whatever is around it
before it begins to build.

to climb to the summit of our soul to raise the flag of victory
letting the mistakes we made together applaud them wildly from below.
I can't tell you how bothered I am by those days
when I raise my head and see right above me the sky
running to hide its sunshines one by one
so I won't see them, won't enjoy them.

Which part of his future would each of us individually see, I wonder
if he could switch on at full power the floodlight of his own honesty?
Maybe this way we could find out how far from our body
our shadow wants to reach.
Or, more likely, how far our kindness can stand to reach
before it starts becoming something that is no longer kind.
For a couple that once again
we both did all we could to find out how deep into the one's kindness
the other's ulterior motive wants to invade
to grab anything good it can use for its own purposes,
the sheets of our bed today will give birth to dozens of faceless questions
so that they'll stop being as soft as they were yesterday.

Our relationship itself will sprout thorns from inside it
to make us feel even more uncomfortable than we already are.
Thus we start walking towards the future
tightly holding in our hands the worse swearwords we have said to each other
while we keep on furiously tearing at the pockets of our memory
regardless if with every step of ours
another happy moment we experienced together drops out of them.

When in a couple one must stop being happy living with himself
to be able to live happily with the other,
then the relationship itself has already crossed its finish line.
Which is the moment in a relationship when the two logics stop constructing
an avenue together so they can reach their common future
and start building two different dirt roads?

Time, which by now is nearly totally corroded,
is emerging from the depths
of the forgotten clock on the opposite wall with slow steps,
steps that no longer remember the orders shouted at them by reality,
only the ones whispered at them
by any ambiguity time allows them to have.
My imperfections just lost the conversational partner they had in me.
Disgusted, I inhale with all the strength in my lungs
the pain of this realization
and begin to throw every one of the next minutes of my life
into the new trashcan my most glittering apology just finished making.

These are the hours in my life
when I wished I was carrying with me the operating manual of my cry.
These are the hours when I wished I could sit a sorrow away from her,
not a reality closer.
The thousand happy moments that time easily just demolished in front of me
began hugging first each other
and then the smallest darknesses they always kept inside them,
and the nights, their greatest expectations.

Armed only with the golden ambiguity
given to me as a gift in the hottest day of summer
by the last emotional winter I survived without the help of my optimism,
I began to tear down the sky above me,
a small light blue piece at a time,
using only the ten most cowardly blows
my courage had inside it.

With every blow I was able to remove yet another joy
until hours later, exhausted by the battle
I surrendered to the brand new, yet intentionally defective courage
which my meanness had made for me in the meantime
and became the February I always hated.
With every blow I felt my fist lose another piece of its truth
until all that I hope for began to fall in love
with what I don't know how to hope for at all.

Tomorrow already started whispering in my ear
in a language I cannot clearly decipher
while I still try to hide my every word my beliefs do not agree with
as far away from my lungs as I can
so that I won't have to say it.

I'm afraid it's time for me to sit at that long blue table
which continuous to be surrounded
by the melody of an otherworldly rage
watching at the only boundary of my life
I deliberately left uninterpreted
my next smile choose to die
before letting my sorrow give birth to it.

I didn't know in which part of my body to hide
so I just hid in my own.
One of my most treasured silences ran after them,
and after hastily glancing at me with an indifferent look,
went past me too.
They frantically ran to find their birthplace.
It's probably somewhere between
the beauty of my own compassion and the sweet and sour flavor
it leaves behind every time it passes over my beliefs.

Death is not the finish of a life,
and certainly not the starting line of another.
It's simply the moment when the smiles and the tears
a person placed in the souls of the people he shared his life with
fall into each other's arms
and together decide to start telling his own story.

Will I manage I wonder to find the necessary amount of courage in me
that will help me run as fast as I can
to have time to become a volunteer castaway
before I'm forced to become a professional lifeguard?
Is this perhaps the check I owe to the death of my cowardice?
Will it let me plant a starting line at my finish
if I betray all the different fragments of my beliefs that never believed in me?
Could this be the realization
that either way I am no longer able to fully fit in my pain,
I cannot fit everything that insists on hurting my soul
into all that aspires to sooth my most ambitious wound?

I have the impression that the biggest part of my own dimensions
is probably saturated by all those "nos" I have been telling it all these years
and decided it no longer wants me inside it.
How the hell do these "nos" manage,
using the mud that I sling on the facade of each of my dreams,
to erase the tracks of my optimism
so that I can't figure out what I feel when I finally manage to dream them?
Maybe the same way that a man's entire future
can shipwreck amid those tough questions
it's been hesitating to ask him all along.

Having for years left my joy unpaid
for what it has offered me my entire life,
I run towards the beginning of my interpretation
and without aiming to, I realize that my passion
has no more excerpts from the meaning of my life
to give as gifts to anyone I loved.
Perhaps the only thing that's left to me
is to become the illicit lover of my ambiguity
before I become the steady date of my own sorrow.

Using the biggest hand I found looking through my body,
I grabbed the smallest truth I found patiently waiting for me next to my past
and with its help began to rip out from inside me
any memory that refuses to remember all I did to forget it.
From a desolate word I wrote a song
the same way the sky makes its body every morning
out of all the blue the night failed to drown in its pessimism.

Remind me not to forget to tell you at the end of the day
all the secrets my truth keeps from me.
Is today the day when lies will no longer be able to choose
the words from which they'll be born?
Playing with the passkeys my intelligence uses
to unlock the hearts that have been reduced to longing for
all that their owners' ambition doesn't allow them to be anymore.

I hope I'll have time to learn how to talk to you
before I forget how to listen to you.
I really like it when I unexpectedly come across someone
whose company I instantly begin to enjoy
with the part of my soul I haven't explored yet.
I have so much need for anything that insists on constantly reminding me
of the reason I still hope.

The way minds start working
when souls submit their resignation letters to their owners.
There is no reality that, looking you in the eyes,
hasn't turned your public image upside down
trying to discover the next truth of yours
that's searching for a way to become a lie.
As soon as your soul heard what I just told you
she refused for the remainder of the conversation
to look in the same direction our future was looking.

A person's first contact with his truth each morning
determines how many clouds the sky will contain throughout the day.
All the apologies I never made
got together for the first time today to apologize to me.
Please let me guide you on a tour of everything I can no longer understand.

by the finish line of the greatest joy in your life.

Do you think that this is the aesthetic of a silence
that demands to be more beautiful than any word of mine?
The time during a conversation when lies take hold of a sledgehammer
and truths a scalpel.
The frame in which my self-awareness puts the day's favorite delusions
and then flashes its prettiest smile to be photographed next to them.

There are words that pierce ears
and silences that pierce consciences.
Would you in the next few minutes
let me wear a much worn lie
and come apologize to our reality?
I threw the next step my convenience brought before me in the trash
and began to roam those paths of my courage
that no longer recognize me.

The day I decided to become a collector of used emotions.
Why do I let my delusions keep the only passkey I have to my happiness?
Dear God, I seem to have forgotten what the sweat of my soul smells like!

Ultimately we are slaves of that part of our character
we hope will free us from the person we became.

that never bothered about their future,
never learned to determine their value
based on how many future moments of happiness
they have already stuffed deep in their own pockets.

These are the memories that were born
by simply plunging into the void
between the wallet where my logic stores her own strength
and the currency that my memory is using
which the next hour of my life
doesn't want to hold in its hands even for a second.

I sit triumphant before my memory's open safe,
not knowing if I should rush to be incorporated
into the least directionless answers
the currency she uses to buy my happiness from me have,
before I'm forced to bury the handshake
her echo has been offering me for hours
in my next dapper yet repugnant mistake
that is coming full speed straight at me.

The time has come for me to confront the inexpressible power my mind has
to convince me that I must remember even what I don't wish to.
Might it be time for me to throw all my troubles
in the face of my own memory?
Might it be time for me to refuse being seduced by the tempest
her own ambition has carefully hidden inside me,
making me forget what I want to remember
so I'll be remembered by all that I want to forget?

How strange! Listening to my memory's rambling triumphs
talk for hours among themselves
I begin to realize that my shortcomings
can easier translate for me all that which, refusing to tell me,
my self-confidence has already confided to them.

My memory does not need my help
to retrieve from the depths of the interpretation of the courage
my self-confidence uses to explain to me how weak she is,
those rusty capabilities of mine that cheerfully spend their hours
playing and balancing on the rim of her favorite trash can,
the one she uses to discard only the most beautiful of my own defeats.

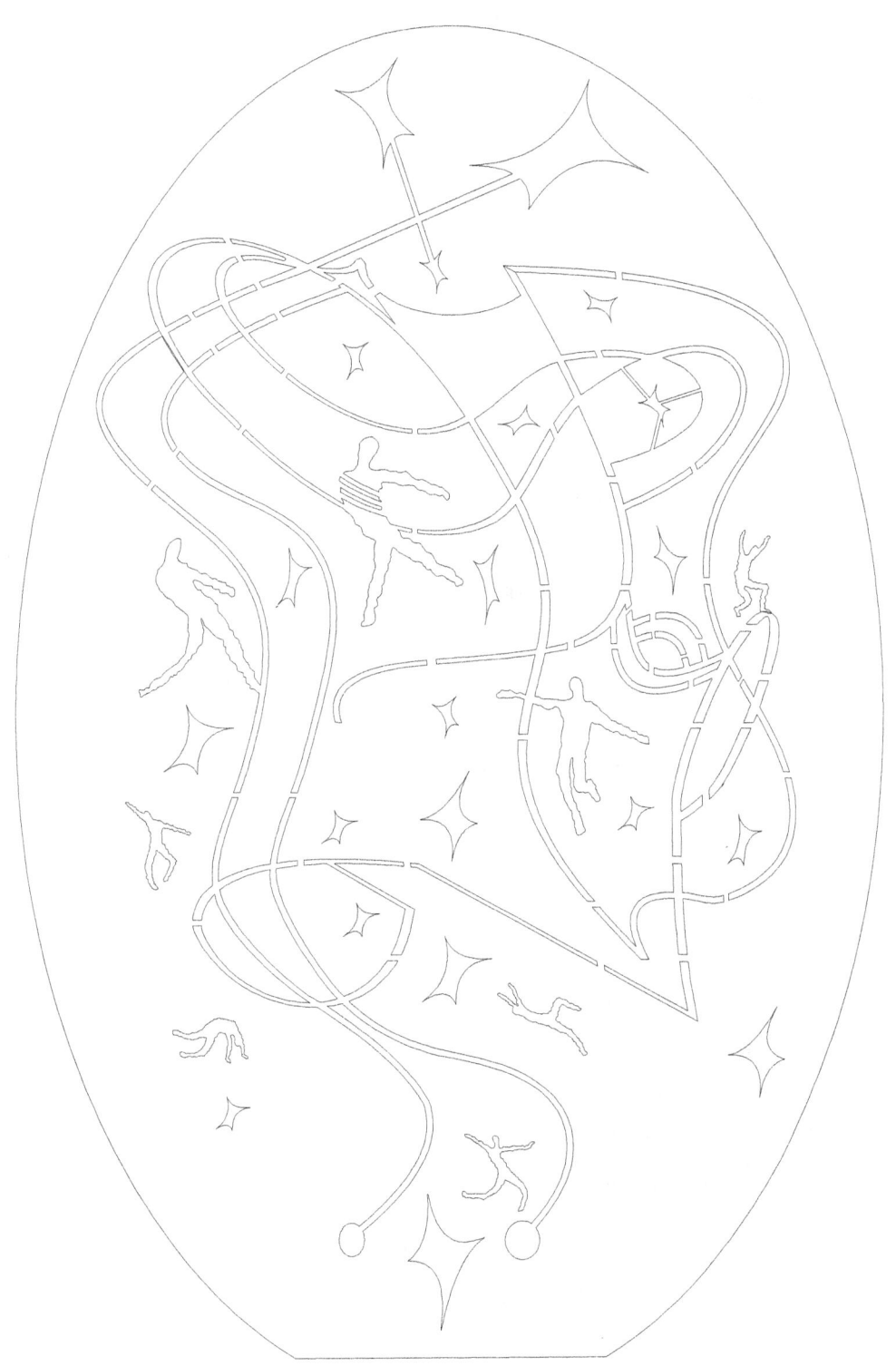

and began in the exact opposite side of my imagination
to intersect any thought of mine that got bored waiting in my brain
and decided to commit suicide
by simply embracing the next silence that would pass before it.

The quickest way to relocate my tenderness,
which is doing its best to avoid looking into my eyes,
is to remain in the same mental state
as my emotionally unshakable stupidity.
So I took all my clothes off,
donned the velvety flavor
of the last enjoyable afternoon I can remember
and went out to meet the limits of my defeatism
hoping I'll finally manage to figure out
what it is they want from me.

I was always impressed by the pain I felt at the end of each day
when I returned from work intellectually sweat-drenched,
feeling as if the meanness of the people I associated with
had gone through my insides with its emotional plow
so that by dawn it could have sown its vicious sperm deep inside me.
When I opened the door to enter my home,
I felt I was already waiting for me there.
I was not alone.
A few feet behind me stood that tyrannical meanness,
ready to throw me on the bed and make love
to any crumbs of my self-confidence
willing to satisfy its desires.

In these moments I learned to choke my day's laughter
in the unbearable strength of the muzzle I wore since childhood,
the one that knew only how to whisper,
but never how to stay silent.

Sedated by her carefully reconstructed grand achievements
my malice wouldn't stop recounting to me,
and while the two of us simultaneously
took part in the seduction of my self-confidence,
I felt her merciless caress searching among the secrets
my body hid in the least visible side of my darknesses
to find the ones that could scare me the most.
Will I be able this way to decipher as soon as possible
the most recent weakness I acquired that day?
I doubt it.

I now feel so small, so insignificant
that I'm willing to imagine
how beautiful it would be to be able to feel
that I could forever escape from the person
I didn't manage to become today.

to indulge my freefall once again.

Dancing with the newborn triumphant lie
I will surrender at the end of the defective verse
which for some minutes now
my ego has been whispering to those pages of my life
which my past has deliberately left blank
so it can fill them out later
putting in them whatever it wants.

I feel the restless eyes of everything I left in my life
without making the slightest effort to understand it
scrutinizing me from head to toe,
not just me but my numerous fears as well.
They are looking to find where the person I used to be went,
where the unreliable porter of my newborn hope has gone,
the one who, trying as hard as he could
to balance on the transparency of his most valid shortcomings,
ended up becoming the guarantor of that part of his luck
that never forgave him for his stupidity.

Dragging behind me with all the strength I have left in me
the echo of my most expensive truth,
I overtook the rest of my image
to be the first to reach tomorrow's front gate.
I just need to manage to enter ahead of my authenticity
without all that I owe her for months now
getting a chance to grab me and keep me from moving ahead.

Waiting on the threshold of my future
watching a few feet away the perpetually unsatisfied questions of my ego
fleetingly banter with my indolent vanity,
which is especially cheerful today,
I realize that I have been living for some time
an uncompromising inch away from the coup de grace of my megalomania.

Is it perhaps time for me to start apologizing to the minor miracle
that lives between the various guilts my logic has
and the remorse contained in my life's meaning?
The poor devil has been waiting for some time now to meet me
in those few moments a person has just seconds after he wakes up
during which he tries to cross the bridge
from the mentally obscure to the emotionally uncertain
without leaving any pieces of his optimism behind.

It's still early in the morning and my logic is trying as always
to find the strength to humiliate before my eyes
everything my soul dreamed of last night.
She is still trying to find a way
to sit me down at an especially uncomfortable school desk
and teach me her own way of understanding it.
Today I will stay awake all night
so that I won't give my pessimism the opportunity

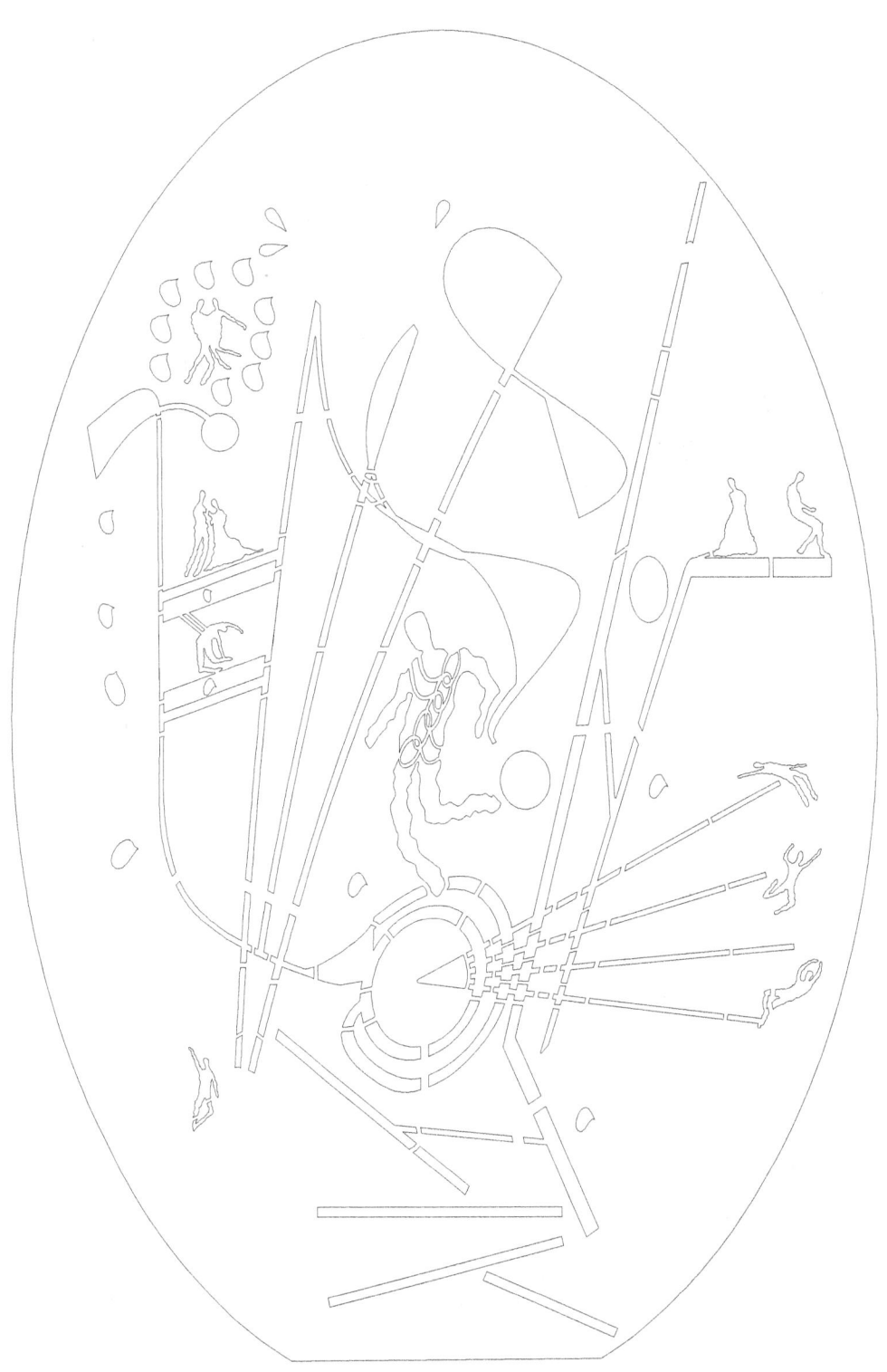

Freed from what I was forced to hope for,
I finally learned how to dream.

Walking towards the part of my happiness
where the back side of my ambiguity ends,
while avoiding to step even an inch into my shadow,
I want so much to be able to fit
into the right dimensions of all that I hope for
without forcing my future to panic.

The kind of absolute silence
that knows how to hide amid absolute bedlam
has come determined to unlock any door inside my brain
which the version of the truth I've hidden inside it
is no longer obliged to open for it.

Cut off from the genuineness
that any heartbeat of mine demands to have,
I survive day by day with the help
of the ten most important doors in my life,
the ones that keep me from discovering
who I should not become.

I feel the pain inside me contracting and expanding
according to which kind of optimism
each of my heartbeats carries within it.
The steep downhill right in front of me,
which for some time now has been looking threateningly at me,
refused to take a step forward, grab me and throw me inside its dreams.
I feel as if I exist simultaneously in two selves,
one who doesn't believe in what he feels
and another who can't feel
what he wants so much to start believe in.

Trying to drop the whole day into my favorite piggy bank
so that I can feel emotionally richer when I enter tomorrow,
I hesitantly drew near this incredibly comfortable armchair
that's sitting alone in the middle of the moon.

When I got to about half a truth away from it
and began undressing myself,
casting away one by one the voluminous footnotes
which all these years my public image carried for me as a favor,
I felt the kind of shadow which my body casts behind it
every time it passes through its own sorrows,
fade away in the middle of the questions it will never dare to ask.

It seems that on the surface of love
the souls that have no reason to fear their own truth
don't allow their most precious emotions, when lighted by the sun,
to cast shadows behind them.

the laughs that refuse to hide behind the operating instructions
handed over to them by the logic of their owners.
Come, let's steal two hapinesses from that part of our pessimism
that's been asking us for years now to teach it how to smile.
Come, let's become the panoramic rewards we will offer our happiness
to let us understand why we are cheerful.
How does one steal two joys out of a sorrow?
By laughing.

Am I ready, I wonder to serve emotions
about which I don't know what part of my logic I must defeat
so she will let me feel them?
I will soon find out.
I will also soon find out how big a part of my self-confidence
my fear insists on concealing within it.
Sensing my happiness touch me on the shoulder
to convince me to stop holding a grudge against her
and start talking to her again,
I saw that the thousand hollow dead ends I felt touching me right then
had already started constructing the next look
with which I will dare to gaze into the eyes
of the handshake my future has been offering me for hours now.

As soon as I finished repairing my happiness
I immediately started creating a sadness.
When I finished making a serenity
I immediately started looking for a reason to feel anxious.
When I finished making an exile
I immediately started building the house I would leave behind.
When I finished with that too
I began to make a self-confidence out of all the times in my life
I chose the first "no" that looked me infatuated in the eyes
over any "maybe" I had to look for a long time in it to uncover.
You see, the entrance to any decision is constantly guarded by a giant "no"
while it's back door by a skinny "maybe".

To shield my loneliness from its very own self
I decided to wrap my next decision
in the alibi I will soon use to acquit the asterisks my happiness placed in my life.
It's interesting how, when you start repairing your compassion
from the attacks of your ulterior motives,
you sooner or later end up manufacturing a scream
so you yourself can hear the apology you want to offer your own life.
It's this scream that to allow you to hear it
will force you to feel all over again
one by one all the parts of the different pains
you have used to produce it.
It seems that man starts believing in his words
only when he stops being in love with them.

it immediately ran to hide in the ruins fogs leave behind them
when they brush past those hearts
that have long lost the right to respect what they feel themselves.

It's probably time for me to ask my rust how much it loves me.
Not knowing what to do next, I started walking aimlessly for hours
around the endless landfill for emotions
that's open twenty four hours a day in the part of my mind
from which I end up not knowing how to get back every time I go there.
After a while I stumbled on a thoroughly abused, almost broken down smile
that would give anything to know again how to feel the emotions it was born to feel.
Happy with my discovery,
I opened my self-criticism's door and got out of my sorrow
to walk on every uphill in my life that owes its slope
to the ambiguity the part of my courage I would use to climb it
always demanded to have.

Will I manage, I wonder, to steal my image from its hypocrisy
the moment I hear it analyze the various excuses it offers me
for preferring to spend its time hanging out with the phony victories
that for years now have been living in my delusions
instead of that kind of draw which I managed to install in my reality
before I started filling it with what would be left of my conscience
if I removed the gifts given to it all these years
by my various injuries?

Trying to build a temporary bridge
to the solutions which hours ago started pushing and shoving each other
to get away from me as quickly as possible,
I hope I'll be able to persuade my strength
to look for a way to breach the borders it shares with my pessimism.

My strength wants so much to be able to find a new technique
to rebuild from scratch my misgivings
which, as soon as they're born, the first thing they'll do
is to embark on teaching me the right way to feel disappointed
before I make the decision to throw myself
into the fight against my own sweat.

Letting your words dig into that soil of my soul
she had never allowed anyone touch before,
not because she was afraid of strange hearts
but because she feared friendly ulterior motives,
I climbed up to the edge of your silence
and stood there defiant for a while
trying to find the courage to ask her what she thinks of me.
What I would not give to have in my possession words
that knew how to dig into the soil of my companion's soul
deep enough so they can plant in her
a kind of love that from the moment it's born will be able
to let her touch the compassion I hide inside me.

What I wouldn't give to every drop of sweat my body uses
to express what I'm no longer able to even think,
to make me feel that my most passionate enthusiasm
has already found a way to communicate with your soul
without my normality being able to overhear what they're saying.

to find the reasons I should never try to feel it.
It's this step I hope to be able to use
to stroll around the beautiful orchards of a relationship
where those thoughts grow
that chose to never adopt an emotional homeland
so they won't ever have to betray it.

at the most important to him spots around his soul,
to shield her from feeling the pain
they themselves want to continue to worship.

The time has come for him to prove to himself
that he can't convince his truth
to attack the emotional sanctuary that is constructed of velvet questions
and whose tasteless wall decor
consists of tens of thousands of one square inch pictures of him.
Each shot was taken the precise moment in each day of his life
when he was more unhappy than at any other.
It's the sanctuary in which cheerful and safe
live those dark feelings of guilt with which he could never negotiate,
since he was never able to convince them
to sit across from him at a table
and talk with him.

Unable to defeat the part of his life
that really wants to be defeated,
he will soon lose the bulk of his authenticity
amidst the numerous alibis offered by his own inadequate excuses.
It's the excuses his sharp mind quickly came up with
to dress his ego with that cherished light blue haze
that knows how to transform any shiny defeat
into a boring and semi-transparent draw.

His last cry unfortunately managed to learn
how to hate the first.
His last silence unfortunately learned very quickly how to love itself
more than it ever loved him.
Sinking in his own anxiety,
he feels the key to his soul spinning like crazy inside him
trying to quickly unlock her in order to discover the shape of the lie
he asked her to manufacture for him.

Anxious, he starts filling his enormous private storm
with as many spare mists he could find right then waiting around
willing to momentarily abandon what they were doing
in order to help him out.
Without losing a second, he starts running as hard as he can
towards the spot where the dream he saw on the first day
he managed to convince himself he was no longer an adolescent
abruptly crashed on the ground of his own ambiguity.

to the simplest thought he ever thought.
Ready to negotiate with the invisible medal
his luck wants to bestow on his most impressive character flaws,
he sits opposite his most cowardly thought
and breaks out in tears.

With one move he uproots from inside him two summers
he had never used before
and gives them to the first person he finds in the street
who believes less in his own arrogance
than in his own intelligence.

I can longer bear to listen to my counterfeit triumphs softly weep
seeing more and more emotional obstacles
grow by the hour all over the body of my self-confidence.

Daybreak will come again today and will lay on my skin
a piece of its most glorious smile
along with the skinniest, yet most optimistic sunbeam it has in its possession.
I hope it will help me catch in my arms,
not only the amazingly powerful fog
which the emergency exit of my cowardice hides behind it,
but also the loneliness of a heart which, no matter how hard she tried,
never managed to pronounce the word "we" properly
without suffering excruciating pain.

I just managed to escape from the last tasteless question
I asked the meaning of my life.
I'm doing everything I can to run away from any worry inside me
which believes that autumn still has the power to decide by itself
when summer will end.

I am thinking of relocating into the echo of the colors
the summer's last day left me when it went away
to introduce itself to the happiness
my pessimism and winter just gave birth to a few hours ago
at the center of my latest defeat.
You see, winter doesn't get born on the last day of autumn,
but in the first minute we start believing that summer won't come soon.

Today I will attempt to go through the rage
the backside of my self-control is generating exclusively for me,
I will dare to go through the second half of my sorrow,
the one that prefers to be shy rather than golden,
so I can be in time to see the dream left for me on my bedstand
by any mental virginity that a whole century of ambiguity
might have left without using to extinguish the fires
my knowledge lit in the middle of my self-esteem.

That charming but malfunctioning century is running to be in time
to engrave the most amorphous doubts it has in its body
on the section of the newborn day that continues to believe
that my imagination will never loan again
any more logic to my logic.

by allowing one's questions to embrace the other's guilt.

I opened the smallest invisible window I could find
searching through the least blue section of the sky
so that everything and everybody I could never love the way I wanted to
could finally come inside me,
became the roommate of my life's last blank page
which refused to synchronize its guilt with my own truth,
loaned a dream to the first drop of pessimism
I saw coming out of my arrogance,
inhaled from the space around my body
all the darkness my misery needs to be able to see me,
and sat in the absolute center of my brain
to try to start creating a soul
out of the gentle rain of all the tears I shed in my life
by allowing my pessimism to produce my own sorrows
before I had the chance to make them myself.

I finally managed to convince my joy
to sit at the same table with my tears
so they can try to explain to her why I cry.
I think I managed to get somewhere after all.

From far away I see my body coming,
lugging on its back the heaviest "I"
it could find searching through the embers of my life.
It can easily bear the weight
because it's my mind that's supplying the muscle, not my body.
It's incredible how much my logic loves her victories
and how much the part of my soul that loves me more
than it loves my own success hates them.

My soul took out of the smallest pocket of her body
the most shy little scarlet darkness you've ever seen
and wrapped it around my eyes so I can't see.
She's been waiting for me for hours
at the edge of the emotionally sterilized parade,
so I can explain to her what happens at the point in a life
when uncontrolled enthusiasm loses its original luster
and turns into a mechanical smile
that has been prepaid by my apathy
to never stop smiling.

Awash in the vertigo of the labyrinthine moment
I tried to grab onto any lifejacket
I hoped my truth would throw me.
But she, dressed in her faceless facade
just sat unmoved a few feet away,
to be exact, a century of all-white guilt away,
refusing to do anything to help me.

No matter how much I tried in my life
I was never able to get into the coin
with which the battle I had just won
paid off my arrogance not to start talking,
not to start explaining to me who she thinks I am.
My sly arrogance always managed to steal my sorrow for a while
giving it back to me twofold
when the echo of my triumph self-dissolved
under the stern gaze of the next reality.
Victory knows so well how to hide at the start of every fight
the pain we will be forced to bear on our back till its end on her behalf.

When did I become the hazy creation
of my triumphs without realizing it?
Letting them mold me for years anyway they wanted,
eventually they decided to lift me in their hands
and place me on this incredibly wretched marble base
telling me that from now on I would live the life of a glorified statue
that is long bankrupt.

the front one, the great star,
the splendor that everybody around me admire so much.

I'm just tired of watching countless people next to me,
and seeing no one.
I'm tired of everyday touching countless minds
and not even one soul!
I want so much to see the person next to me
separated from the shining echo of his victories,
isolated from the carnivorous stillness of his defeats.
I want to see the person next to me for who he is,
not a marionette dressed in the dazzlingly ridiculous outfit
which his character strengths force him to be dressed in,
or the unbearably heavy shadow
which his defeats force him to carry all day behind him.
Why can't we understand that our shadow becomes more difficult to carry
the more of our own virtues we toss inside it?

From afar every victory looks like an omnipotent smile.
Up close it looks like an inexplicable injury.

that I'm coming!
Going up the first fearful step of the day
which is gradually appearing out of the morning dew,
I feel as if I am being followed
by the thousands of sweat drops I have shed in recent years,
which, forming the saddest waiting line I have ever seen in my life,
are trying to collect from each day that goes by
an advance on my future serenity.

Beside me also walk all those hopes
that I never let quarrel with my past
even when they tried to defend me during the relentless attacks
it decided to launch at me from time to time.

Ah, I still remember those beautiful hopes
I had in those days when my smile every morning
was made exclusively for me by the freshness contained
in the first baby truth the sun brought me and laid on my knees,
and not the copy of yesterday's smile
which every day I wearily picked up along with my keys
from the hallway table before going to work.

It is there that the distorted by my own ambition questions
which the shadow of the previous day neglected to ask me
never forgot to leave that copy of a smile.
That crafty shadow, knowing I would never be able to answer them,
stuck them one by one on the surface of the bathroom mirror
so that I wouldn't be able to avoid entering a new day
without giving them a chance to humiliate me once more.

It took me quite some time to realize
that only very few of the journeys my mind takes
end up being as free of charge as they seemed at their start!
My poor soul always ends up paying for my mind's mistakes
because the blows a person suffers from his own shadow
are far more powerful and merciless
than the blows of his strongest opponent.

Accompanied by the pleasure a person feels
when he manages to feel stronger than his biggest nightmare
and weaker than his saddest sorrow,
I continued to carefreely traverse my day
walking through the successive keyholes
that yesterday had given to me as a gift.

You see, I wanted to convince my image
to become so perfect so as to resemble as best it could
the smallest mistake I am interested in making today.

Trying to be the awkward acrobat of your soul for yet another day,
I unwittingly get trapped in my mind's morning haze.
I anxiously try to find a way to open the window
facing the biggest worry I have about the future
without being seen by my shortcomings, but I can't.
Meanwhile, dawn runs like mad
to ask anyone it finds around me except me
to tell it what it should believe in today,
which flag to raise over the heads of the people it will illuminate
to prove to the others, but most of all to itself,
that it still has enough soul in it to keep on fighting for what it believes in.

There, in front of the only window of reality
your optimism has left half open
I stand ready to learn from scratch
the new spelling the coming day demands to use
to describe me to my vanity.
This is the spelling I want to use to persuade my tongue
to write on the next thought I will have about you
with words of its own choosing
what is left in my life every time I stop enjoying my joy,
what is left on the surface of my heart
when I stop asking her why she is so unhappy.

When my tongue manages to do that
I would like, before it starts writing on the next sentence that comes out of my mouth,
to realize which part of the meaning of my life
is the one it makes me leave on the edge of the blade
my serenity uses to cut the thousands of ropes
with which my pessimism has tied me to my future.
How odd! Man is so willing to surrender to his future
the thousands of ropes he will ask it himself to tie him hand and foot with
so he won't become something different
than what he promised his vanity he would be!

Closing my eyes as tightly as I can
and inhaling with my every breath those of my shortcomings
I refuse to admit that they are mine
I start, by using the instinct my survival briefly lends me,
placing them back one by one
in the part of my logic where they were born.

I am finally ready to break into all I hoped for until yesterday
to be able to hear to the last every secret
my courage wants to confess to those beams of the sun
which came to listen to the harmless grumbling expressed
in the almost mythical song
my favorite darkness has been humming for a while now.
I hope that by casting as much light as they can spare from their battle with the night
on those parts of my life that need it most,
they'll help me find the answers to those semi-transparent questions
my feelings for you want for months now to ask me.

I have built myself in the middle of my mind
read "Freedom"?

Long ago a mean thought of mine,
at a time when, regretting all it had done to me,
it was slowly dying in the arms of a major defeat, told me:
"Whatever you do in your life
make sure that your soul is your ally
because if it is only your logic that agrees with everything you do
at some point you will be called upon to fight to the death
with your very happiness."

It was so right!
Man cannot fight with his principles
without ending up fighting with the person he wants to be.
Because no matter how logical whatever he does is,
no matter how compliant with the rules
with which he has tightly wrapped the reality in which he lives,
at some point of his courage he will falter, he will stop
and, as long as he keeps on moving forward obeying only the rules of his logic
while pretending that he doesn't hear what his soul is whispering to him,
the more he will hurt and suffer.

May I confess something to you?
Unfortunately, I have reached a point of not knowing
how to tear myself away from the beginning of every thought of mine
and take the suspended step toward the end of every act of mine.
I don't know how to turn my back on who I am
and rush to thrust into the embrace of who I want to be.

How I wish as soon as I took my favorite full stop out of my pocket,
the one I always used whenever the next word I had in my head
refused to sprint to my mouth,
I could stumble on the beginning of what I wanted to think about!
I guess this is the happiness of living in a world
where the full stops in your life refuse to put an end
and have come back to roost in your mind
begging you to teach them how to survive in a happiness
that wants to forget how to end.

to come into my life through that window of my soul
my damn sorrow built right across from my greatest triumph.
Meanwhile, for the first time in a long while
I feel almost ready to claim back those emotions of mine
I never managed to introduce to my enthusiasm
before my defeatism got to know them first.

Living for so long in the luxury
enjoyed by an honesty that has chosen by itself the final dimensions
it will attain in the mind of its owner,
I start using the most misspelled thoughts my optimism contains
to be able to reach the edge of my mouth.
There I wish I could finally read
the words my hopes left for me
shortly after the end of the last battle I lost
without ever being able to figure out what I believed in while I was fighting.

As many as the number of his own truths that he himself killed.
Oh, how much I like to use those facades of mine
like the two-sided jackets I have
which, when one side gets dirty
the other comes to save my truth
from the image it sees when it's forced to look at me.

I now feel ready again to start hearing inside me
what my most discreet silences
wanted to confide to me all these years,
the ones that always lived in that most inhospitable space
that exists between my lips and the toxic echo
left behind by my last great anger.

So I threw myself inside the blue and white key
which will try to find, among the myriad locks
that each of my worries is using to protect itself from me,
the one that wants to open least of all.
Seeing it struggling to consume its truth as fast as it can
I was able to touch the ultimate agony a darkness can feel
when it is forced to watch the birth of a dazzling flame right next to it.

Ready to collapse mentally,
with the little strength I had left in me
I began to wrap around my angriest tears
any of the darknesses near me that didn't want to voluntarily enter
into what I was trying to feel at the time.

A triumphant guilt away,
those words of mine that were still trying to learn
how to stand up to the incredible power of the very silence
that has not finished yet negotiating with my own cowardice
came to testify against that purple sorrow
which kneeling awaits my life to give it absolution.

I ask my knees if they can bear to carry the weight
of the myriad apologies I need to quickly start fabricating,
but I don't get an answer.
All I can see is most of my life's keys smile
realizing the absolute power they have
to determine the importance of the dimensions of the door they just opened.
What do you call a dream that refuses to wake up with you in the morning?

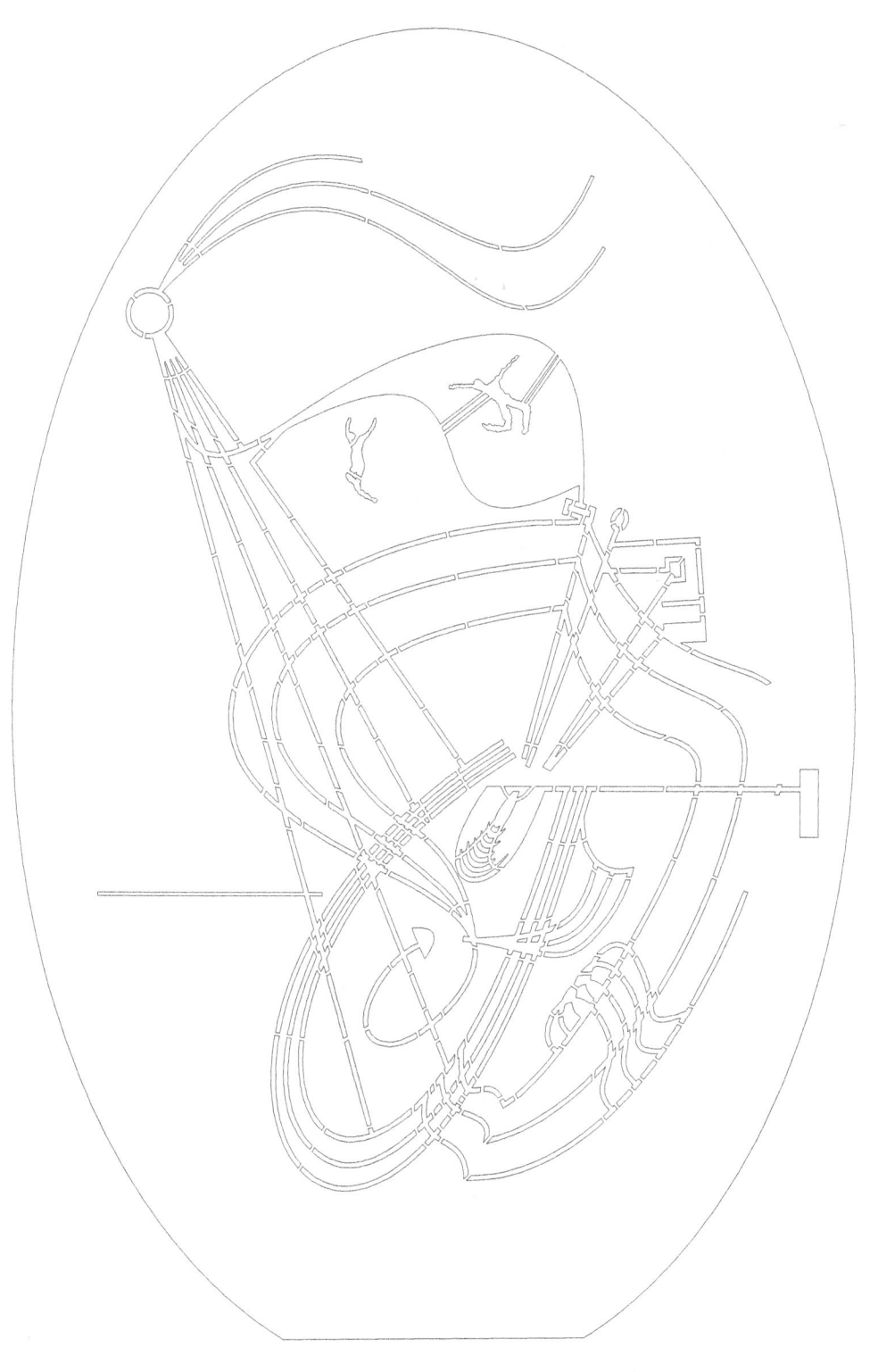

emitting that dreadful odor of self-rescinding impasses.
The dictatorship of loneliness in which he lives
forces him daily to traumatize
everything that the fingers of his soul want to touch
before he tries to understand what it is that he is feeling.
Granting his greed the sacrosanctity
of all the things he wanted to do since childhood,
he taught his hopes to daily supply his soul
with dreams whose expiration date has already passed.

Who is really eager, anyway, to get to know the badly-lit corners of his soul
before the ever playful truth grabs them and throws them at his feet?
The ambitious ulterior motives know so well
how to dismember the future of their owner
before they are forced to understand
what it is that their own future is trying to tell them.
They are so good at devising those half-transparent smiles
to avoid the craven translation
of the meanness they so cleverly know how to hide within them.

As long as his own smile prefers to stay
two plastic seductions away from him,
he continues with great success to humiliate in advance,
not only every hour of his life before it even begins,
but also the next reason
that will try to make him feel really happy.
This way he believes that he will manage to avoid for yet another day
having to explain to himself why he can't afford the cost of being kind.

He managed to become the fanatical enemy
of the one sunbeam that still believes in him,
the person who ends up at the close of each day
begging from those nooses of impunity
that never stopped swinging like a pendulum inside his head
for any crumb of serenity they are willing to give him.

They are the ones which he himself cannot casually feel,
though the people around him never stop assuring him
that every time his meanness takes the steering wheel of his life from his hands,
they see those nooses of impunity
carelessly crossing the street his words are walking on
so they can go and hide in the spot inside him
where his courage goes to find sanctuary
every time it gets frightened.
The damned things believe that only they have the right
to translate everything they touch
into a soul that can no longer read the subtitles
she herself is putting in his own dreams.

How the details of my life like to get tangled in my feet
to stop me from being able to decide!
I have the impression that the dream
the night has already strung around my neck
won't ever realize that I've been impatiently waiting since this morning,
unable to dream it,
and even more unable to not dream it.
Disappointed, it keeps on squeezing me hard
until it makes me realize
that, if it wanted to, it could even choke me.
I wonder, what happens to a dream of yours
that you will never manage to dream?
It becomes the back side of your next reality.

I whisper, I don't speak. I feel. I don't think.
I feel so I don't have to think.
I walk backwards so I don't have to remember.
I move forward so that I don't stumble on my disillusionment.

It's daybreak and my shortcomings are already trying
to fit in the first look the mirror will soon give me
bypassing my eyes and going straight to the back part of my mind,
the part of my body that insists on waking every morning
later than my truth.
Once again the poor thing is struggling to learn from scratch
how to think the way they taught it
and not the way it wants.
By God, it's so disappointing as soon as you wake up
to hear your shortcomings be the first to wish you good morning!

Leaving the shelter built by the golden refuge in my mind
so it won't come into contact with me each time I run to hide inside it,
I slammed the rusty door of reality in my soul's face
and felt, for some reason I can't explain,
that before even trying to do something today
I'm already in debt to my most accomplished shortcomings.

I owe to explain to them
why I will believe in the handcuffs they will put on me themselves
more than in the freedom my good qualities
have been promising for days they'll give me.
Those little rascals insist on wanting to kidnap me from my very day
if I ever manage to persuade my sorrow to move aside even for a moment
and let me give birth to my serenity!
Now I understand why two people start fighting
when one's shortcomings begin to believe
more in the adversary than in their owner.
I must face it.
There are no handcuffs that like to be generous
because there is no freedom that wants to be tightfisted!

that belongs to the life across from me
knows so well how to deconstruct those minutes of the day
that no longer want to be part of my life.
Meanwhile, the pieces of my ambiguity
which I don't know how to define anymore
have been standing for some time right in front of me
begging me to let them be the alibi of my stupidity.

Without being able to understand why I refuse right then
to pay what I owe to my next body,
I struggle to comprehend the magnitude of all that I hesitate to hope for.
It's not an easy thing for me.
The most transparent lie I keep in the closet
where I store my collection of various half-truths
has already tied around my leg
the heaviest ambiguity it found while searching through my honesty.
The only thing that remains for me to do
is to try to consume the vagueness of my image as quickly as I can
before you begin to realize how phony it is.

I have no other kinds of compensation to offer to my authenticity
in exchange for her silence.
My favorite lie, this marvelous interpreter of my own truth,
just started negotiating directly
with all those questions you had about me,
the ones you chose to make out of a material
that looks like stainless steel silk
to avoid making them out of promises which will quickly rust
when exposed to the rain of the reality your beliefs live in.

All these years I've been regularly seducing my own image.
Now the time has come for me to feel its defiant master key
seeking to negotiate with the part of my serenity
that wants to be more sustainable, even if it can't be self-reliant.
I feel that I am the result of a life that learned early on
that, to make my ego happy,
I must become something more than a coward
and something less than a hero.

Long persecuted by my own cowardice
I now come and stand in front of you,
wearing only my most ambitious deformity.
I am a fugitive from my own insecurity,
an improvised human patch
made from the most emotionally expensive material that exists in the world,
a truth that has decided from now on to tell only lies.

I came to ask you to teach me
how, by taking off as fast as I can the mask with which I've covered my brain
so that I won't have enough time to lie to the first half of my soul,
I'll be able to convince the other half
to allow me to start feeling again.

which found a way to live in my future before me.
Many would like to be able to demolish it
before it gets a chance to teach me how to enjoy it
by simply understanding what it will never become.

Midday has already started transforming itself
into the spacious weakness of mine where my sorrow will stay today.
So I began to unload the doubts of my optimism
on the first thought which, embracing me,
managed to tolerate the odor of my truth
without turning her eyes away in disgust.

I don't have a single spare purple darkness left.
I sold them all.
I even sold the last hug my body manufactured today
to the first worry that found again the courage
to believe in the power of my smallest smile.

So I became my laughter's velvety traveling companion
who with the enormous eraser given to him by the time that remains in my life
came to help my anxiety learn from scratch
how to erase the darkest black
that has decided to move to the center of my next serenity
by using all the leftovers of white it still has in it.

When I let my soul free to dream
there is no white that goes to waste.
Seated at the smartest edge of my own stupidity
I am finally able to realize how much happiness I still have in me
which I never had the courage to start exploring.
Daybreak no longer gasps for breath while trying to figure out
how many things I've asked it to do on my behalf today.

Maybe happiness means to be able to stand being in love
with your most perfect imperfections.
With this in mind, I realize that I should let my logic fall in love
with every dream I will never be able to see.
I took a running leap into the void
between the wind that did everything in its power
to leap out of the deepest, most optimistic sections of the sky to come find me,
and the spot where my body will be in a minute.

Lies are not born in the mouths of those who tell them
but in the ears of those who believe them.
Today I have ten joys to throw into every answer I will give
to the questions my silence feels obliged to ask me.

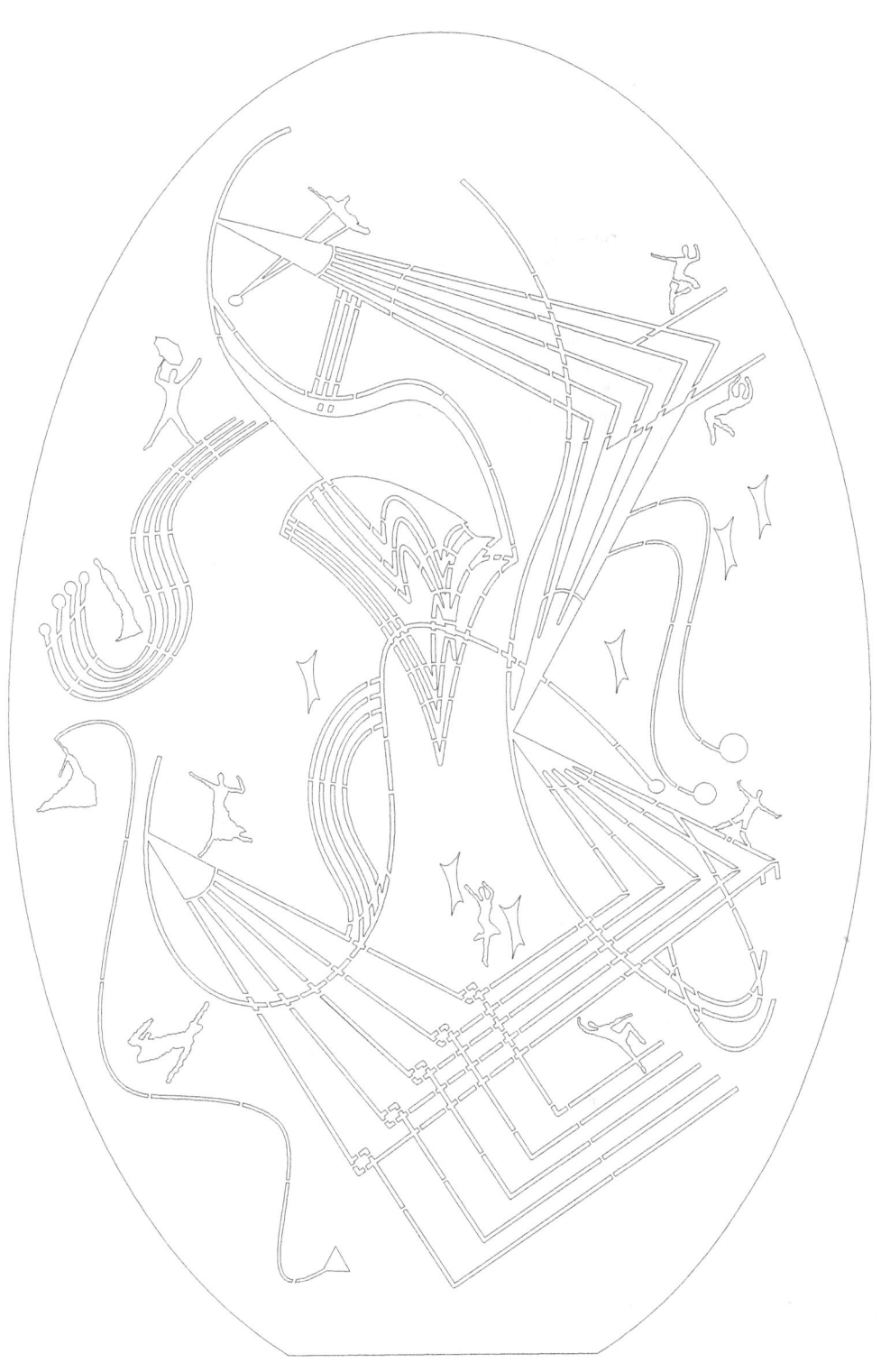

I saw out of the corner of my eye a few feet behind
a tiny desert trying to enter my life without me detecting it.

At that moment I became the warden of my day's fifth hour
during which I was able to realize that every new lie
that I don't believe intends to lie to me
deposits on the skin of my soul
yet another charmingly invisible layer of mud,
the type of mud that is able to instantly transform my soul
into an unrecognizable amorphous question
that not even I can recognize anymore.

My soul demands to be left to live within her own truth,
as far away as possible from the machinations of the lies of my logic
with which she wants to constantly dress her,
to make her more presentable,
so that my ulterior motives are able to use her
to secure the victories they seek.

The difference between a soul and a mind
is that the latter also sells lies.
A soul does not know how to lie,
does not know how to adjust what she wants to feel
to make it more acceptable, more appealing, or even more comfortable,
all she wants is to be left alone to live in the absolute light of truth
which she gives birth to every minute.
A soul does not use currency in her transactions,
does not just obsess about how to climb the next step of the ladder,
she simply wants to proclaim to the world around her what she believes in.
She doesn't bother about the price she will be asked to pay
so the next minute will allow her to cross it
without any help from the various techniques
that logic has invented to make the road more comfortable.

Logic, this extremely capable peddler,
the great admiral of lies and seductive pirate of honesty,
is constantly trying to sell to the people around me
what she herself is able to understand
from what my soul told her that she feels.
It bothers me so much that it's so rare for one to be able to find out
exactly what the soul of the person he's talking to really wants to say.
In most cases one may only hear what the other person's words say,
which have been taught by logic
how to transform what his soul wants to express
into something more practical, more self-serving, more phonily luminous.

What a shame that the middleman of my authenticity
is depriving you of the ability to clearly see what I have in me,
the ability to feel what I feel,
to touch the truth that lives inside me.
Instead of that, the only thing you can see
is an often nicely packaged, minimally spontaneous view of my true self
honed through time by my logic,
which has managed to round off all the sharp corners
that rip the truths that dare brush by them.
A viewpoint which, having already raped those honesties
that are not consistent with some ulterior motive,
eventually makes two people offer one another
only the small part of themselves
which is already approved by the part of their ego
that lives permanently in their own lies.

So I end up offering myself at a permanent discount
hiding the truth that insists on being truthful,
the truth that does not match the one that people around me want to buy.
While I'm doing that, I get used to my new image
and start feeling more comfortable
with being the person that I sell to others
rather than the one I end up selling to myself.
How happy must the person be who sells to others
nothing different than what he is trying to sell to himself!

I admire my soul, which after all these years
still doesn't know how to create a slogan, or pass along a message,
doesn't know how to flatter, has no ambitions,
doesn't think about next steps and next triumphs,
only cares about how she can faithfully express
the truth I have inside me.
A mind lives for the future,
the soul only for the very moment she is experiencing.
No matter how many hours a person spends in his lifetime thinking about his future
he will never be able to feel
even the simplest emotion that belongs to his next minute.

We admire a flower that adorns our life,
but the soil it's planted in is the truth that gives it life and beauty.
Beauty has an expiration date, but truth doesn't.
Maybe that's why nature made the flowers beautiful but evanescent.
The soil has a different kind of beauty,
the dignity of an inexhaustible strength
which continues to generate beauty because it knows how to generate truth.
I don't know. Somehow I always thought that truth was my life's soil
and my image was its flower.

Back cover painting
I ask the sunset but it won't answer me:
Why is the truth in love with the perimeter of the great lie?

www.ingramcontent.com/pod-product-compliance
Lightning Source LLC
Chambersburg PA
CBHW081455040426
42446CB00016B/3249